AN IRISH
FLORILEGIUM II

AN IRISH FLORILEGIUM II

Wild and Garden Plants of Ireland

Watercolour Paintings by Wendy Walsh

Introduction and Notes on the Plates by Charles Nelson

with 48 colour plates

THAMES AND HUDSON

We dedicate
this entire Florilegium
to all those who in past centuries have
explored the flora of Ireland and enriched her gardens,
and especially in this tercentenary year to the botanists and gardeners
who have been associated with the botanical gardens
of Trinity College, University of Dublin,
from 1687 to 1987

Wendy Walsh   *Charles Nelson*

*Any copy of this book issued by the publisher as a paperback
is sold subject to the condition that it shall not by way of
trade or otherwise be lent, resold, hired out or otherwise
circulated without the publisher's prior consent in any form
of binding or cover other than that in which it is published
and without a similar condition including these words being
imposed on a subsequent purchaser.*

© *1987 Thames and Hudson Ltd, London*

*All Rights Reserved. No part of this publication may be
reproduced or transmitted in any form or by any means,
electronic or mechanical, including photocopy, recording or
any other information storage and retrieval system, without
prior permission in writing from the publisher.*

Printed and bound in Japan

CONTENTS

ACKNOWLEDGMENTS 6

FOREWORD by Dr W. A. Watts 7
(Provost of Trinity College, Dublin)

INTRODUCTION 8

THE PLATES 17

LIST OF PLATES 210

BIBLIOGRAPHY 212

INDEX 214

ACKNOWLEDGMENTS

We extend our thanks to all those who have helped us in one way or another in the course of our work on this second volume of *An Irish Florilegium*.

As in the original volume, those who provided plants for painting are individually acknowledged in the Notes accompanying each plate, and we must again express our appreciation to the Director of the National Botanic Gardens, Glasnevin, Dublin, for granting facilities for our research as well as many of the flowers depicted herein.

The publication of *An Irish Florilegium II* was most generously supported by

Irish Garden Plant Society

University College, Cork

Ulster Television

World Wildlife Fund

University of Dublin, Trinity College

Miss Sybil Connolly

Dr Neil Murray

A. W. B. Vincent

John J. Brogan

For their munificence we express our personal gratitude.

November 1986   W.F.W. and E.C.N.

FOREWORD

It is an honour to be asked to write the Foreword to *An Irish Florilegium II*. The first volume, splendidly illustrated by Wendy Walsh, celebrated famous Irish plants and famous garden plants introduced to cultivation by Irish collectors and gardeners. This time the underlying theme is the succession of botanic gardens at Trinity College, the first of which was established three centuries ago in 1687. Charles Nelson's scholarly introduction follows the history of the gardens from their first role as sources of material for the training of medical students to being pleasurable places to display plants to the public, and finally to places where some of the flood of newly discovered plants of the nineteenth century were brought into cultivation and new varieties, hybrids or cultivars produced for the pleasure of gardeners. Old prints of the College show a formal garden with geometric walks and trimmed hedges near the Provost's House, but this did not survive into the nineteenth century. Dr Nelson shows that Trinity's great period of plant introduction and horticulture had come to an end in this century when the competing claims of new sciences reduced the role of taxonomy and of a teaching botanic garden in the College's Department of Botany. The present garden at Dartry maintains good collections, preserves endangered species and continues to give pleasure and instruction.

I should take this opportunity to pay tribute to Wendy Walsh whose beautiful flower portraits have attracted much admiration in recent years. She originally developed her natural talents under the guidance of a Japanese master while she was resident in that country and learned his skills and the materials he used. Family considerations delayed the development of her career and she returned to plant illustration by producing designs for stamps first in the Gilbert and Ellice Islands and then in Ireland where she had returned. Whole series of illustrations of remarkable Irish plants, animals, fish and marine life followed, contributing importantly to the already high artistic quality of our postage stamps. Her first major collection appeared in *An Irish Florilegium*. We must be grateful that such a talent is available to us in draughtsmanship and in freshness of colour. I wish the new volume a deserved success.

W. A. Watts
Provost

20 November 1986

INTRODUCTION

The paintings in this second volume of *An Irish Florilegium* continue the themes of the initial work. The abbreviation AIF I refers to the first volume, published by Thames and Hudson in 1983.

The first sixteen plates portray plants that are truly native species in Ireland or, like *Fuchsia magellanica* (Plate 12) and *Allium babingtonii* (Plate 9), long-established aliens. Two of the indigenous plants – *Rosa* × *hibernica* (Plate 1) and *Carex buxbaumii* (Plate 2) – are now extinct in their wild habitats but they do survive, although somewhat precariously, in botanical gardens and in the gardens of a few enthusiastic plantsmen.

The second group of thirteen paintings represents exotic species that were discovered in distant places or were introduced into cultivation in Europe by Irish botanists and gardeners. Moreover, the botanical epithets of four of these plants commemorate eminent Irish botanists, Michael Pakenham Edgeworth (*Primula edgeworthii*: Plate 17), Dr Samuel Litton (*Littonia modesta*: Plate 24), Dr David Moore (*Crinum moorei*: Plate 23) and Dr James Townsend Mackay (*Mackaya bella*: Plate 25). The latter two were closely connected with the College Botanic Garden last century.

The final set of nineteen plates depicts some of the superb cultivars associated with Irish nurserymen and gardeners, including the winter cherry (Plate 47) introduced by Daisy Hill Nursery, Newry, County Down, which was established by Tom Smith one century ago in 1887. To mark the outstanding work of Irish rose-breeders, our final picture (Plate 48) portrays one of the unique single-flowered hybrid-tea roses from the Dickson family, who began their unequalled work of breeding new roses at Newtownards, County Down, in 1879 and offered for sale their first cultivars one hundred years ago in 1887.

But the cultivars chosen for this volume span a longer time, almost two centuries, from the early 1800s when Edward Hodgins raised a hybrid holly (*Ilex* × *altaclerensis* 'Hendersonii': Plate 42) in County Wicklow to the present year when the new virus-transformed cultivar *Pelargonium* 'Koko' (Plate 45) is to be released from University College, Cork. This new plant demonstrates that Irish horticulture is still lively and advances in the vanguard of the science, proficient in the modern techniques of plant breeding.

As before, the choice of each subject was determined by our personal predilections and perhaps our prejudices. Thus, for example, we have chosen again an 'old-fashioned' rose rather than a modern cultivar, but we do not mean thereby to suggest that the plants rejected are no less worthy of portrayal. When we have been deliberately exclusive it was for a purpose, and that was to mark in this anthology the singular contributions of three establishments to botany and horticulture in Ireland and further afield: Daisy Hill Nursery of Newry and Dickson Nurseries of Newtownards (both in Northern Ireland) and the Botanic Garden of the University of Dublin. Their stories are encapsulated in the following pages and paintings.

The First Botanical Gardens in Europe

The vitality of botany and horticulture in Ireland owes much to the work of the botanical gardens that have flourished and, it must be admitted, withered here during more than three hundred years. They served as focal points, stimulating the exploration of Ireland's native vegetation, acting as trial grounds for new imports and, most significantly, functioning as centres from which novel plants were distributed freely to other gardens and to a host of amateur gardeners.

But what distinguishes a botanical garden from other gardens which also fulfil those roles? The traditional and still-accepted definition is that a botanical garden is a place in which is cultivated as wide a selection of plants as possible given the limitations imposed by space, climate and soil. Particular plants are grown because of their intrinsic botanical interest and not for their imagined beauty, although any botanical garden in which plants are well grown will have its own beauty and give pleasure. Thus the pursuit of knowledge is the primary purpose of a botanical garden; its beauty is merely the consequence of the good cultivation of an immensely varied assembly of plants. In contemporary terms, this special emphasis means that these gardens are centres of botanical and horticultural research and also of education. An eighteenth-century poet, Abel Evans, put it succinctly when he wrote that the University of Oxford's Botanic Garden was 'For Knowledge, as for Pleasure Made'.

The academic role is inherited from the garden which was formed at the University of Pisa, Italy, in 1543; it was created to serve as a place in which the students of physic (the archaic term for medicine) could be taught to recognize the many plants used in the preparation of medicines. The Pisa garden is regarded as having been the first botanical garden in the modern sense, although many of its characteristics, including its basic ground plan, were clearly derived from the gardens of medicinal herbs planted in the monasteries of medieval Europe. The link between medicine and botany is, however, much older and goes far back into antiquity, to the herb-gatherers who jealously guarded the secret lore about the properties of the plants they collected in meadows and woods. That immemorial connection also explains why the earliest botanical gardens were called physic gardens or medicinal gardens (*hortus physicus*, *hortus medicus*).

The lead given by Pisa was soon followed by other Italian universities: Padua in 1545 and then Florence (also 1545) and Bologna (1547). A physic garden was formed in Zurich in 1560, in Leipzig (1579) and in the Netherlands at Leiden in 1587. In that year, on St Patrick's Day (17 March) several of the governors of the University of Leiden requested that an empty plot of land, situated behind the university, should be ceded to them so that a garden for the instruction of the students of medicine could be planted. The City Council of Leiden agreed to this on 13 April. Eleven days after that, the governors raised the salary of Geraert de Bont by 50 guilders on condition that he taught the medical students about plants during the summer months. In February 1589, de Bont was replaced as Professor of Medicine and Botany by Pieter Pauw, who had been one of the University's first students of medicine. But nothing much else happened and no garden was actually formed until Charles de l'Ecluse (Clusius), who was appointed *Praefectus Horti* (Director) in 1592, and the gardener (*Hortulanus*) Dirck Outgaertszoon Cluyt planned and began planting a small patch in September 1594. Despite its meagre dimensions (about 40 metres by 31 metres), they cultivated almost one thousand different species and varieties of plants. L'Ecluse's original sketch-plan survives and from it his garden has been reconstructed; the original ground is still part of the present-day Botanic Garden, which covers about 50 hectares. During the last four centuries, Leiden Botanic Garden has not only served its university and city, but it has had a remarkable influence on botany and botanical gardens throughout the world, including Ireland.

The first botanical garden in Britain was created at the behest of Lord Danvers at the University of Oxford in 1621. Almost half a century elapsed before another was formed, this time in Edinburgh (1670), followed three years later by the famous Physic Garden of the Society of Apothecaries in Chelsea. Both the Oxford and Chelsea gardens survive on their original sites, but in Edinburgh the garden has moved several times to different plots – the present Royal Botanic Garden in Edinburgh was begun only in 1820.

When the University of Leiden was granted that vacant land in 1587 there was no university in Ireland. Queen Elizabeth was on the throne. The whole island was troubled – a rebellion had been crushed in Munster, Ulster was far from quiet and there were threats of foreign intervention – threats which seemed real in the following year when the Armada set sail from Spain. Yet the English administration was slowly subjecting Ireland to its authority and Dublin, a growing and prosperous town, was the home of many educated and cultured men. In 1591, prompted by several of its more learned citizens, the Corporation of Dublin set aside the lands occupied by the derelict Priory of All Hallows for use as the site of a university. A royal charter was sought and on 3 March 1592 the College of the Holy and Undivided Trinity near Dublin – *Collegium Sanctae et Individuae Trinitatis juxta Dublin* – was incorporated as the 'mother of a university'. Thus the University of Dublin, comprising a single college, came into being. Today it is commonly known as 'T.C.D.' or, colloquially, 'Trinity'.

T.C.D. – The First Garden

For many decades the curriculum in Trinity College, Dublin, was directed solely towards producing graduates who proceeded to enter the Church. Not until the latter part of the seventeenth century did the study of medicine become a concern of the University. Dr John Stearne was made Professor of Physic in 1662, but on his death in 1669 the professorship was left in abeyance until about 1700 and there was no active Faculty of Medicine. Despite this, on 25 June 1687 the Board of Trinity College decided that a physic garden should be established. The kitchen garden, which hitherto had supplied vegetables for the Fellows and scholars, was taken over for the purpose and work began almost immediately on converting it to its new role. There is no record of a curator being appointed; instead, the gardener employed to look after the campus had to take on the extra work, and his salary was increased by 20 shillings per quarter because of his new responsibilities. From the College archives we learn that a weeding-woman, Margaret Armstrong, was engaged and that she was paid 10 pence for one day's work 'mending the ditch'. It is not, however, certain where this garden was on the campus.

This first Physic Garden survived the vandalism that occurred when the troops of King James I occupied the College campus in 1689 and 1690. It was not carefully maintained, but the site was not forgotten. By 1701 the Physic Garden was restored to its proper purpose, and throughout the next decade was weeded, planted with new shrubs and kept tidy. No records have been preserved of the plants grown in it during these early years, nor does a plan survive.

The College flourished in the early eighteenth century. Medical teaching was firmly established as a part of the curriculum, and Dr Thomas Molyneux was appointed Professor of Physic on 22 January 1711, replacing Dr Richard Stephens 'lately deceased'. A new era was thus ushered in and better teaching facilities were provided for the School of Physic; between June 1710 and August 1711 an 'Anatomie Theatre' with a laboratory was built on ground 'laid out at ye south-east corner of the physic garden...'.

Thomas Molyneux was a graduate of the University of Leiden; he was a student there in August 1683 when Paul Hermann was the incumbent *Praefectus Horti* and he would undoubtedly have studied the plants in Leiden Botanic Garden. As Professor of Physic in Trinity College, Dr Molyneux was responsible for engaging a lecturer to teach botany, and he was fortunate to find another graduate of Leiden, Dr Henry Nicholson, to undertake that task. A native of County Roscommon, Nicholson was a frustrated student of law; he had enrolled at the University of Oxford but was refused a degree three times. In January 1709 he travelled to the University of Leiden and six months later graduated. While in Leiden he met Hermann Boerhaave, the most famous of the Leiden botanists, and was later to obtain seeds from him for Dublin's Physic Garden.

Dr Nicholson delivered a botanical lecture when the Anatomy Theatre was opened on 16 August 1711. In October that year he wrote to the English botanist John Petiver, saying that he had undertaken the task of replanting the Physic Garden and expanding the plant collections, and asked Petiver for seeds. Nicholson wrote a small booklet about the arrangement of the plants in the garden – *Methodus plantarum in Horto Medico Collegii Dublinensis* . . . (1712) – but a career in law was still his dream, and in 1715 he left Dublin for London.

T.C.D. – The Second Garden

No successor as 'Professor in Botanie' was appointed, as far as we can ascertain, until about December 1724, when another Leiden graduate, Dr William Stephens, took over Nicholson's post.

Meanwhile, much building was taking place on the campus. The magnificent new Library was begun on 12 May 1712, and work continued for twenty years until its completion. For a reason which has not been discovered – it may have been something to do with the building of the new Library – it became necessary in 1723 to abandon the old Physic Garden and to create a new one. The site of this second garden was 'behind the Library', between the Anatomy Theatre and Nassau Street. William Maple was in charge of the removal of the plants from the original site to the new walled garden. By the spring of 1725 all the plants were safely transferred and the College was justly proud of its new Physic Garden. It even advertised that 'The Physic Garden . . . will be opened on Monday 1 June 1725, and a course of Botany will be there begun to continue every Monday, Wednesday and Friday.' Admission was by ticket.

We do not know how successful this venture was, but the lecturer was almost certainly Dr William Stephens. One of Stephens's other undertakings was the preparation of a catalogue of the collections, a job which he completed by October 1726. The extant catalogue shows that Dublin's small Physic Garden contained both native and exotic plants, including rare African *Pelargonium* and *Aloe* species most probably obtained from Holland.

The rectangular, walled Physic Garden served Stephens well. He gave lectures there to the students of physic, but clearly he was bored by the need to repeat the same lectures year after year so he published his notes in the form of a remarkable little book, *Botanical elements . . . for the use of the Botany School in the University of Dublin* (1727). In it he acknowledged that plants had male and female sexual organs, a fact that few other botanists would have been prepared to accept at that time; but Stephens had been well taught at Leiden by the incomparable Hermann Boerhaave.

Dr Stephens resigned as Professor of Botany in 1733 when he was appointed Lecturer in Chemistry. His place was taken briefly by Dr Charles Chemys, but after a few months, in September 1733, Dr William Clement succeeded to the Chair of Botany. Little seems to have happened during Clement's term; the Physic Garden was maintained usually by a single gardener whose wages are recorded in the College accounts. In 1763, Clement resigned as Professor of Botany – by this time he was Vice-Provost of Trinity College – and was replaced by James Span. Dr Span supervised the gardener who weeded the beds in the Physic Garden and tended its plants, but nothing has been discovered about the state of the garden nor about the vitality of botany in the College during these years. Span died in 1773; he had been popular in the University and was one of the Dublin physicians elegized in a strange poem by John Gilbourne.

Dr Edward Hill was appointed Professor of Botany in his stead. From his own writings we learn that Hill inherited a Physic Garden in which was a single barren fig tree tended by an ancient gardener, the whole overshadowed by lofty elms. The offal from the Anatomy Laboratory, according to Hill's lurid account, was thrown out into the Physic Garden, where it was devoured by ten thousand rats! Not a happy state of affairs and not conducive to the cultivation of plants or the teaching of botany.

T.C.D. – The Third Garden

Dr Hill was extraordinarily single-minded and so tenacious of his dreams that he had the ability to make himself thoroughly unpopular. He soon abandoned the rat-infested Physic Garden with its barren fig and began a long campaign to have a new garden established. He tried to have other ground on the campus set aside for his project, but the Board of Trinity College refused. And there is no evidence that he (or his predecessors) ever had a garden in the square now called Botany Bay; that College landmark was, I suggest, named after the penal colony.

Unfortunately for Hill, the struggle was protracted and there were many disappointments, many stumbling-blocks. Furthermore, there were other men, not connected with the University, intent on the same purpose. On 9 February 1790 a petition was tabled in the Irish House of Commons which resulted in a grant of £300 to the Dublin Society for the formation of a public botanical garden. The Dublin Society invited the University to cooperate in forming a botanical garden, but the Board of the College declined. The Parliament's objective was achieved when, on 25 March 1795, the Dublin Society obtained land at Glasnevin and began forming the botanical garden that is now the National Botanic Gardens.

Despite many frustrations, Dr Hill did not give up, and when the Provost, John Hely Hutchinson, died in 1794, Hill seized his chance to wrest from the successor, Dr Richard Murray, verbal consent to lease a plot of land in his own name on behalf of the University. Edward Hill found a suitable site possessing 'natural advantages, infinitely above all that any Botanic Garden in Europe can have to boast of' at Harold's Cross, which was in those days one of Dublin's outer suburbs, and he signed the lease. He began almost immediately the labour of creating a new garden; basic work was commenced and a house was built for the curator, but funds were restricted. Hill was forced to spend large amounts of his own money on the new Botany Garden and he was given little support by the University. In the end, a change to the statutes governing medical education in Ireland forced Professor Hill to decide whether he would keep the Chair of Botany or the Chair of Physic – he held both – and he resigned the botanical one. Thus he gave up his grandiose garden plans: his 'fond imaginings [of] ten thousand trees and shrubs and flowers, by care and art made denizens of a climate not their own' evaporated.

An unseemly row ensued over the Harold's Cross Botany Garden. Dr Hill took the University to the High Court, and in 1803 the King's Bench awarded him possession of the land at Harold's Cross and full compensation for the money he had spent, but he was instructed to release the College from the lease.

Meanwhile the University had appointed a new Professor of Botany, Dr Robert Scott, and for two years it was Professor Scott who had the problem of looking after the Harold's Cross Botany Garden.

T.C.D. – The Ballsbridge Garden

When the battle between Dr Hill and the University was concluded, the Harold's Cross Botany Garden ceased to exist, but the derelict Anatomy Garden (the second Physic Garden) was still available. The Board of the University had given permission for Professor Scott to employ a gardener and assistant to supply specimens for lectures, and it was thus that James Townsend Mackay came to Dublin from Scotland and took up the post of College gardener and botanical assistant on 25 March 1804. He was given charge of the College grounds and the old Anatomy Garden, but it was most unsuitable for a botanical garden and new grounds were sought. On 5 July 1806, Trinity College undertook a lease for 175 years of land owned by Lord Fitzwilliam in Ballsbridge, and James Mackay set about creating the College's fourth and most famous botanical garden. Ground work started in the autumn of 1806, but major planting was not undertaken until 1808.

The College Botanic Garden at Ballsbridge was eleven years younger than the Dublin Society's Botanic Gardens at Glasnevin, but within two decades Mackay created a garden that excelled the older one. He established a fine collection of exotic shrubs and reported that many supposedly tender plants could grow out-of-doors at Ballsbridge. A list that he published in 1825 demonstrates the richness of the Garden's collections; included were *Correa alba* from Australia, the mudan (*Paeonia suffruticosa*) from China and *Aristotelia macqui* from Chile. *Fuchsia magellanica* (Plate 12) also flourished and James Mackay noted that it was 'now very common in gardens'. At this time Glasnevin was in decline under the ageing and hardly competent Professor Walter Wade. The Society, which had adopted the title Royal Dublin Society in 1820, was stifled by petty internal squabbles and cared little for its botanical garden. When Wade died in 1825, it was even suggested that James Mackay should be invited to superintend both of the Dublin botanical gardens; but that never happened and Glasnevin's decline continued until 1834, when another Scot, Ninian Niven, took charge and arrested the dilapidation. From that time Glasnevin and Ballsbridge engaged in friendly rivalry, a competition enhanced in November 1838 when James Mackay's fellow-countryman, one-time pupil and former foreman, David Moore, became the Curator at Glasnevin.

Mackay's reign at Ballsbridge lasted for fifty-six years, until his death in 1862. He is best remembered for his remarkable contribution to the study of Ireland's native flora, which culminated in the publication of *Flora Hibernica* in 1836; the field-work for this *Flora* was done at the College's expense, beginning in 1804. As for his contribution to horticulture, Mackay introduced many plants into Ireland through Ballsbridge, including the eponymous orchid *Zygopetalum mackayi*. The College Garden gained a substantial reputation for growing difficult subjects, including the Western Australian pitcher plant *Cephalotus follicularis*, and (later under John Bain) the lace plant from Madagascar (*Ouvirandra fenestralis*). During Mackay's curatorship and the terms of his successors, numerous fine plants were sent from Ballsbridge to London for portrayal in *Curtis's Botanical Magazine* (founded in 1787 and thus two hundred years old). *Sida picta* (from South America), *Helleborus lividus* from Majorca (Plate 29), *Brachyglottis repanda* (from New Zealand), *Androsace lanuginosa* (a Himalayan alpine plant) and *Amorphophallus kerrii* (from Thailand) are just a few of the Trinity plants depicted in 'Bot. Mag.' between 1827 and 1924.

Mackay's other great contribution was in training young men as gardeners; he had the skill to imbue them with both horticultural expertise and an acute botanical sense. His most famous pupil was David Moore, whose work at Glasnevin from 1838 until 1879 raised that botanical garden to a position of primacy among the world's great botanic gardens. Charles Moore, David's younger brother, was another of Mackay's pupils; he served as Director of the Royal Botanic Gardens, Sydney, from 1848 until 1896.

By the mid-1800s Trinity College, Dublin, had become one of Europe's great botanical centres by virtue of the presence there of two men. James Townsend Mackay was widely respected as a horticulturist and field botanist; the University of Dublin acknowledged this by awarding him an honorary doctorate in 1850. His colleague, the Professor of Botany, William Henry Harvey, was the world authority on the taxonomy of seaweeds and the flora of southern Africa, whence came the beautiful genus named *Mackaya* (Plate 25) in honour of Dr Mackay. Harvey was also Professor of Botany to the Royal Dublin Society, and was thus closely connected with the two rival botanical gardens.

James Mackay died on 25 February 1862. The new Curator of the College Botanic Garden was his assistant, John Bain, another highly competent gardener of Scottish descent. Bain was plagued by ill health and retired in 1868; but in 1873 it was announced that he had returned to duty in Ballsbridge. He maintained the high standards set by Mackay and continued the exchange of plants between Glasnevin and Trinity. But in October 1875, ill health forced Bain finally to retire and for a short time the curatorship was occupied by Michael Dowd, who had trained at Glasnevin. However, the task was too onerous for him and he had the good sense to resign, making way for a young man who was learning his craft in the University of Leiden Botanic Garden.

Frederick William Moore, son of Dr David Moore of Glasnevin, was only twenty years old when he returned to Dublin as Curator of the College Botanic Garden in November 1877. His father had sent him to school in Hanover and then to work in Van Houtte's nursery at Ghent. After that apprenticeship, in May 1876, Frederick Moore moved to Leiden and worked in the Botanic Gardens while attending the botanical lectures given by Professor Willem Suringar, Geraert de Bont's sixteenth successor as *Praefectus Horti*. But the young Moore's term at Ballsbridge ended as abruptly as it had begun; when his father died in June 1879 he was appointed Curator of the Royal Botanic Gardens, Glasnevin. Sir Frederick Moore (knighted in 1911) was the most revered of Glasnevin's directors; he remained there until his retirement in 1922, ending the Moores' reign of eighty-four years.

The College Botanic Garden was much smaller than Glasnevin, hardly 8 acres compared with 48 acres, yet it possessed the same basic facilities and grew many of the same plants. There were especially fine hollies, *Magnolia* shrubs flourished despite the smoke of city chimneys, *Arbutus unedo* (the native strawberry tree) and the giant 'rhubarb' (*Gunnera manicata*) from South America survived out-of-doors without protection. It contained many valuable plants; in the 1890s two grass-trees from Australia (*Xanthorrhoea*) were particularly admired and there was a fine early-flowering daffodil called 'Trinity College Maximus' that was made famous by the next Curator, Frederick William Burbidge.

A native of Leicestershire, Burbidge was a gardener with a literary flair; he had been employed on William Robinson's periodical *The Garden* between 1873 and 1877, and before undertaking the curatorship of the College Botanic Garden he had published books on a variety of topics, ranging from botanical drawing and cool-house orchids to domestic floriculture and daffodils. In 1877, on behalf of Messrs Veitch, Frederick Burbidge travelled to Borneo, where he collected, among other things, a ginger that was named after him (*Burbidgea nitida*) and the famous carnivorous pitcher plant (*Nepenthes rajah*) which was soon flourishing at Glasnevin. At Trinity he continued writing, and thanks to him we have some of the finest descriptions of Irish gardens in the last decades of the nineteenth century. Burbidge encouraged many amateur gardeners in Ireland – Mrs Alice Lawrenson (*alias* Saint Brigid: Plate 30) was one who benefited from his friendship. Indeed, there was a perceptible change of emphasis in the College Garden, away from pure botany into ornamental horticulture. Being fascinated by such genera as *Galanthus*, *Helleborus* (Plate 29) and *Narcissus*, Burbidge built up collections of them and engaged in protracted, frequently witty, arguments about the origins of their cultivars in the horticultural press.

In 1892, when the University celebrated its tercentenary, the College Botanic Garden received many plaudits – 'without undue boasting, it may fairly claim to be, in proportion to its size and general conveniences, a garden as rich in vegetation of all kinds as exists elsewhere in Europe'. There was also a gift, a tree-fern from Victoria (Australia) which was supposed to be about the same age as the University. *Todea barbara* had been dislodged 'after much difficulty' from a ravine; it weighed 3000 pounds (1360 kilograms) and was shipped to Dublin in a crate. The fern was not the only botanical gift; Baron Ferdinand von Mueller, who had had *Todea barbara* wrenched from its native habitat, named another Australian plant after the Provost, Dr George Salmon (*Velleia salmoniana*: Goodeniaceae).

After Frederick Burbidge's death on 24 December 1905, the post of Curator was abolished. Care of the College Botanic Garden was undertaken by a foreman under the direction of the Professor of Botany. Hitherto the Curator had been responsible only to the Board of the University and thus was independent of the Professor: William Harvey did not interfere during Mackay's term, nor did Edward Percival Wright during Burbidge's tenure. Professor Wright retired in 1904 and was succeeded by Dr Henry Dixon. The head gardener in Burbidge's place was S. G. Wild.

The departure of Frederick Burbidge had one other immediate result – the College Botanic Garden vanished from the pages of the horticultural press! It became a secluded backwater, and a slow, gradual senescence began.

Like its companion sciences, botany is continually changing. At the beginning of this century, the emphasis swung away from taxonomic work towards experimental and field botany. The College Botanic Garden became less relevant to the teaching and research of the University's School of Botany, and more and more expensive to maintain; unlike the National Botanic Gardens at Glasnevin, the College Botanic Garden has never been supported by grants from the state and there were more important calls on the University's own limited finances. Moreover, the Botanic Garden was separated from the main campus and therefore not easily accessible to the Fellows and students who were entitled to use it for study or simply for quiet recreation. In contrast to Glasnevin, the College Botanic Garden was not generally open to members of the public, although they were admitted on application to the University.

In the early 1960s, there was much of beauty and interest in this secluded Botanic Garden. *Crinum moorei* (Plate 23) flourished in the order beds, and three massive, gnarled specimens of *Testudinaria elephantipes* shared one of the glasshouses with a fine collection of saxifrages (Plate 5), a particular research interest of Professor David Webb. *Helleborus lividus* (Plate 29) survived in the shade of the trees, while an ancient *Wisteria sinensis* clambered up an old *Cordyline*. The Orchid House, although reduced in size, contained many unusual species – the centenary tree-fern flourished there too – and the rockery was 'presided over' by a venerable plant of *Pachystegia insignis*.

As the lease was to expire in 1981, the College decided not to renew the arrangement and to dismantle its fourth and longest-surviving botanical garden. The work was undertaken during 1968 by Dennis McKennedy, who had succeeded S. G. Wild and Bob Byrne as foreman.

T.C.D. – The Fifth Garden

A small site was set aside at Trinity Hall, adjoining Palmerston Park, for the formation of the College's fifth Botanic Garden. Some of the plants from Ballsbridge were moved into new greenhouses and beds. Others, including Baron von Mueller's 'peace offering', *Todea barbara*, were donated to the National Botanic Gardens, Glasnevin. Sadly, the College Botanic Garden at Ballsbridge ceased to exist and its site is now 'graced' by two luxury hotels –

a few of the holm oaks and other trees, and the surrounding stone walls surmounted by iron railings, still betray an oasis that long ago was Glasnevin's friendly rival.

The new, compact Botanic Garden fulfils the old role – it is 'for Knowledge made'. There is a laboratory for the use of students, and growth-rooms in which the temperature and day-length can be controlled precisely, thus allowing the University's botanists to conduct research on plant physiology. Order beds have been remade and they closely resemble – by chance, I think – those of the first botanical garden at Pisa; they are rectangular plots separated by gravel paths and edged with neatly clipped dwarf box and tiles.

Although the pursuit of knowledge is no longer closely linked with the pleasures of cultivating a beautiful garden, this small, functional garden with its modern technology does not disgrace its predecessors. Indeed, the adventurous spirit of Frederick Burbidge, James Mackay and William Stephens has been rekindled. A collection of the rarer native Irish plants is maintained – the Killarney fern (*Trichomanes speciosum*: AIF I: Plate 5), the globe flower (*Trollius europaeus*: Plate 14) and saxifrages (Plate 5) are examples. And endangered species from other countries are now a special concern of the School of Botany in Trinity College, Dublin.

In 1985, Dr Peter Wyse Jackson (Administrator of the College Botanic Garden) and Dr John Parnell embarked on an expedition to Mauritius with Dr Quentin Cronk of the University of Cambridge. Their purpose was to attempt to propagate some of that island's endangered flora. The expedition was a considerable success, and in the Botanic Garden several extremely rare Mauritian endemics are now growing vigorously. The beautiful red-flowered ebony *Trochetia boutoniana* is reduced to no more than one hundred plants in its native habitat, but the Trinity team succeeded in rooting cuttings. (By coincidence, *Trochetia blackburniana* from St Helena flourished in the Ballsbridge garden in the 1890s.) *Elaeocarpus bojeri* just survives on Mauritius; only five plants are known, but eighteen cuttings were rooted, increasing the population more than fourfold. There is but a single plant of the bottle palm *Hyophorbe amaricaulis* left alive; the Dublin and Cambridge botanists are hopeful that they have saved it from extinction too.

The work of Dr Jackson and his colleagues should preserve those Mauritian plants from the fate that befell the island's most famous inhabitant, the dodo. That is a most propitious beginning to the fourth century, a remarkable achievement for the fifth Botanic Garden of Trinity College, Dublin.

Floreat!

November 1986

E. CHARLES NELSON
National Botanic Gardens, Glasnevin

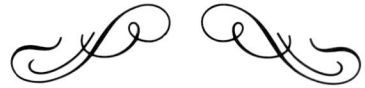

PLATE I

Rosa × hibernica Templeton

PLATE 1
Rosa × *hibernica* Templeton

Rosaceae   Irish rose, ros gaelach

There are perhaps two hundred and fifty species of *Rosa* distributed throughout the northern hemisphere and twelve are listed in the current census of Ireland's native flora.

Wild roses frequently interbreed and hybrids occur spontaneously in the wild. It is generally believed that *R.* × *hibernica* is such a hybrid, the progeny of a dog rose (*R. canina* L.) and a burnet rose (*R. pimpinellifolia* L.), both of which are indigenous to Ireland.

The Irish rose was first collected by the renowned Belfast naturalist John Templeton in 1795 near Holywood in County Down; he reported that he had seen *R.* × *hibernica* in two other places, one near Belfast and one at Magilligan in County Londonderry. Today the Irish rose is probably extinct in the wild — certainly it has not been collected for many years at Holywood, and no-one has been able to confirm beyond doubt the rose's occurrence at any of the other reported sites in Ireland and Britain. Thankfully, this Irish hybrid survives in a few gardens and it is now being propagated, so it is not in danger of total extinction.

The plants from which the sprays were taken as models for the painting have a significant history. The habitat of *R.* × *hibernica* at Holywood was well known to botanists during the nineteenth century, but urban expansion slowly reduced it until, by the middle of the present century, it was thought to be extinct. However, Professor J. Heslop-Harrison found one plant near the Holywood railway station in 1955, and by the early 1960s this too was threatened. To save it, Robert Johnston transplanted the bush to the Experimental Garden belonging to the Department of Botany, Queen's University, Belfast, and that plant still lives. The flowering spray came from it. At my request, Robert Johnston propagated the rose, and a number of young plants were made available; one of these was planted in my own garden at Celbridge, County Kildare, and a second was donated to the Department of Plant Science, University College, Cork, where the modern techniques of micropropagation are being employed to increase the rose further.

Rosa × *hibernica* has been in cultivation for almost two centuries. John Templeton was as keen a gardener as he was a field botanist, and he grew it at Cranmore, his small estate in the Malone district south of Belfast city centre. He sent young plants to fellow gardeners in London and to the two botanical gardens in Dublin. Templeton meticulously recorded the rose's performance each year in his diaries, and from these notes we know that it bloomed for a long period. In one year, 1809, the Irish rose came into flower on 31 May and was still bearing a few blossoms on 13 November.

Like the dog rose, one of its supposed parents, the Irish rose forms a tall, thorny shrub — the plant at Queen's University, Belfast, is over 4 m tall and as broad. It does not send out far-flung suckers. The shoots are armed with stout, straight and slightly curved thorns, and very young shoots also have fine, hair-like spines. A pleasing character of the rose is the grey-green foliage, and each leaf is composed of five or seven leaflets, which have a sparse covering of hairs beneath, especially on the veins. The flowers closely resemble those of the dog rose, having five heart-shaped petals, pale pink fading towards the centre with a bright, creamy-yellow base. The five sepals have serrated margins and long, broadened tips. In the centre of each bloom is a cluster of yellow stamens, their anthers turning brown after anthesis. *R.* × *hibernica* has dark, cherry-red heps which were succinctly described by John Templeton as being 'inverse pear-shaped', and they bear a crown of persistent sepals — in *R. canina* the globose heps are orange-scarlet and the sepals are deciduous, while in *R. pimpinellifolia* the heps are black and the sepals are not deciduous.

Rosa × *hibernica* does not betray its hybrid origins clearly. It resembles most closely the dog rose and shows few characteristics inherited from the burnet rose, which is the dwarf, suckering rose of Ireland's coastal dunes and limestone pavements. But the genetic systems of roses are complicated and hybrids tend to resemble the seed parent (their mother plant) more closely than their pollen parent (their father plant) —

continued on page 20

---

1 Cultivated in Department of Botany Experimental Garden, Queen's University, Belfast, County Antrim (flowering shoot), 20 June 1984, and by Dr E. C. Nelson, Celbridge, County Kildare (fruiting shoot), 20 September 1985. [×0.6]
Figures in square brackets indicate the reduction of each original watercolour from life-size.

continued

rarely do hybrid roses fall halfway between their parents – and thus it is suggested that *R. canina* was the seed parent of *R.* × *hibernica*. In the 1950s, Gordon Rowley succeeded in raising plants from a dog rose (*R. canina* ssp. *dumetorum* (Thuill.) Keller & Gams) pollinated by a burnet rose, and he reported that these artificial hybrids closely resembled the wild stock of the Irish rose, but had 'a more dwarf [*R. pimpinellifolia*]-like habit'. While such experiments cannot prove the suggested parentage of John Templeton's rose, there is general agreement among botanists that *R.* × *hibernica* is a hybrid.

The Irish rose can be cultivated in any garden; it is hardy and lime-tolerant. Some English nurseries have sold plants under the name *R.* × *hibernica*, but they have not been correct; scions can now be made available of the authentic plant. The artificially produced hybrids have apparently not survived in cultivation.

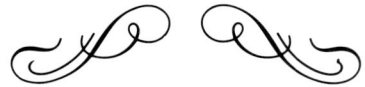

PLATE 2

Carex buxbaumii Wahlenburg

PLATE 2
Carex buxbaumii Wahlenburg

Cyperaceae   club sedge, cib ghorm

This sedge is extinct in its one recorded wild habitat in Ireland; like *Rosa × hibernica* (Plate 1), it survives only in gardens and the cultivated stock is derived vegetatively from the original population.

In Britain, *Carex buxbaumii* is reported from two localities near Inverness in the north of Scotland, but it occurs throughout the northern hemisphere in the cooler, wetter regions. A fen plant in Scotland, it grows with *Phragmites australis* (Cav.) Steud., several other sedges, and the cotton-grass *Eriophorum angustifolium* Honck.

The discovery of this sedge in Ireland was one of the achievements of David Moore when he was engaged by the Ordnance Survey to study the botany of counties Antrim and Londonderry after 1834. He collected *C. buxbaumii* in July 1835 on a small island, called Harbour Island, at Toomebridge in the northwestern corner of Lough Neagh. At about the same time, David Moore discovered a grass *Calamagrostis stricta* (Timm) Koel. (northern small-reed) which, while still growing in the wild, is confined to the shores of Lough Neagh – it is a protected plant. Both these plants were beautifully drawn and coloured by George du Noyer; his illustrations were printed in the second edition of the Ordnance Survey's *Memoir of the ... parish of Templemore* published in 1837.

Carex buxbaumii was already a very rare plant when David Moore discovered it in 1835. Joseph Woods saw it at Toomebridge in 1855 and S. A. Stewart collected specimens in June 1867. On 27 June 1886, just over a hundred years ago, Stewart recorded 'one little patch about two feet square ... trampled down and eaten by cattle' – that was the last occasion on which this sedge is known to have been seen growing wild in Ireland. Grazing and the cutting of brushwood from the little island so altered its habitat that the sedge became extinct.

David Moore was partly responsible for the species' rapid decline because, like many other botanists at that time, he collected enough material to make about a dozen herbarium specimens and also living plants for botanical gardens. Plants were sent to the College Botanic Garden and Glasnevin Botanic Gardens in Dublin, to William Hooker at the University of Glasgow and probably to others also. The plant used for this plate came through Donal Synnott from Arthur Stelfox, who was well known as a cultivator of Irish native plants. Stelfox probably acquired his stock from the National Botanic Gardens, Glasnevin, where the sedge was certainly cultivated for more than a century.

The Lough Neagh sedge's Irish name is cib ghorm – the blue sedge – a more descriptive name than the English, which is club sedge. The young keeled leaves have a very distinctive blue (glaucous) sheen; when mature the leaves are about 60 cm long. They emerge in a tuft from the short, creeping rhizome, and from this also comes the tall, erect flowering stem. All species of *Carex* are characterized by sharply triangular stems, and this one is no exception. At the tip of the stem there are from three to five separate, cylindrical spikes, each one composed of numerous minute, unisexual flowers; the uppermost spike has female flowers at the top and male flowers at the base, but all the other, lower, spikes consist only of female flowers. Each male flower is composed of reddish-black glumes (scale-like structures) and three stamens which dangle from the spike when they are ripe. The female flowers have dark-brown glumes which enclose the single green ovary crowned by three filamentous stigmas.

Carex buxbaumii is easy to cultivate. It thrives in a peaty soil, and will tolerate relatively dry conditions – it does not need to be grown in a bog or water garden. Once established, it will quickly spread to form a substantial colony.

2 Cultivated by Mrs W. F. Walsh, Lusk, County Dublin, 5 July 1985 (small flowering spike, 6 June 1985). [×0.65]

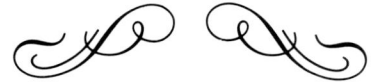

PLATE 3

Lathyrus japonicus Willdenow

ssp. *maritimus* (Linnaeus) P. W. Ball

PLATE 3

Lathyrus japonicus Willdenow
ssp. *maritimus* (Linnaeus) P. W. Ball

Papilionaceae   sea pea, peasairim thra

The sea pea is one of Ireland's rarest wild plants and is fully protected under the Wildlife Act of 1976 (Flora (Protection) Order 1980). In Ireland it is a plant of sandy beaches, growing above the stormline, but in other parts of Europe it is more frequently a colonizer of shingle beaches. At the time of writing (1986), no mature plant of *Lathyrus japonicus* is known to be growing in the wild in Ireland, so the painting was done using a cultivated plant. In cultivation the sea pea becomes more lush than in its windswept habitats among the sand dunes fronting the Atlantic Ocean.

However, the plant depicted has a life-story which turns the whole question of conserving native plants on its head – it was grown from an unknown seed collected on one of our western beaches.

In the last few years, a group of dedicated beachcombers in Ireland and Cornwall have accumulated new information on the frequency of seeds and fruits stranded on our Atlantic coastlines. Hitherto it was said that these 'drift-seeds' were rare and unusual objects, but it is quite possible in a few hours, after a westerly gale, to find several hundred seeds on a single beach – on 1 April 1986 at Hayle in Cornwall, with the assistance of Larry Williams, I found 107 seeds of five different species, and on 2 April 1986 at Perran Sands, with Des and Roger Lidstone, 113 seeds of nine different species. On both these occasions seeds of *L. japonicus* were found in quantity (24 and 19 specimens respectively).

Thus, seeds of this plant are frequently stranded on the beaches of western Ireland and Britain, but there are so few seed-bearing plants of the sea pea known at the present time in those regions that questions have to be asked about the origin of those seeds. Seeds of *L. japonicus* have been recorded from three Irish beaches – Derrynane in County Kerry, Fanore in County Clare and Malinbeg in County Donegal – and from several widely separated beaches on the British mainland (Hayle, Perran Sands and St Ives, all in Cornwall) and in the Outer Hebrides (Barra). Undoubtedly, seeds are also stranded as frequently and in as large numbers on hundreds of other beaches on the Atlantic shores of these islands.

The seeds are viable; specimens from Cornish and Irish beaches has been germinated and the plants grown to maturity. A plant raised from a seed collected by Larry Williams on Hayle beach flowered in 1985 under the care of Des and Roger Lidstone. The plant grown from a seed collected in County Clare flowered for the first time in 1986, and this is the plant shown in our plate.

Where did the seeds come from? As there are no mature, seed-bearing plants growing on Irish coasts at this time, none of the seeds stranded on Irish beaches can be of Irish origin. There are no mature plants growing in western and northern Cornwall, nor are plants at present known on Barra; again the seeds cannot be of local origin.

Fruits and seeds from tropical America are stranded on the same beaches on which the seeds of *L. japonicus* have been found – indeed, the seeds of this plant are invariably found beside such tropical drift-seeds as nickar nuts (*Caesalpinia bonduc* (L.) Roxb.), sea beans (*Mucuna sloanei* Fawc. & Rendl.) and sea hearts (*Entada gigas* L.). The inescapable conclusions are that the seeds of *L. japonicus* also came from the Americas and that they have drifted across the Atlantic Ocean.

The corollary of that statement is that the sea pea is not a rare and declining indigenous plant, struggling to survive on Irish and British coasts, but that it is an occasional and frequent immigrant which will reappear from time to time as long as American seeds continue to reach western beaches. It could be argued that the extensive populations of the sea pea growing in eastern Britain and on the coasts of other countries bordering the North Sea, as well as the shores of the English Channel, are the sources of these seeds, but the currents of the North Sea and English Channel do not generally feed flotsam on to the western shores of Britain and Ireland.

Lathyrus japonicus is a perennial herb with a deep rootstock that may extend for at least 2 m

continued on page 28

3 Cultivated by Dr E. C. Nelson, Celbridge, County Kildare, 20 June 1986. [×0.85]

continued

into the sand or shingle. From this rootstock pale, grey-green stems emerge which are tinted red. The leaves are also grey-green, composed of about four pairs of ovate leaflets arranged in opposite rank along the rachis, which ends with a coiled tendril that serves as an anchor to hold the stems relatively steady in the face of ocean gales and as a means of climbing if the plant is in a sheltered place. The flowers are produced in midsummer, arranged in an inflorescence, the main stem of which is up to 7 cm long. Each flower is pea-like, about 2 cm long, with petals shaded from crimson to purple and blue. Like all leguminous plants, the fruits are pods and these contain about six spherical seeds just like miniature peas, greenish-brown or deep tan in colour and with a distinct linear hilum extending about one-third of the way around the circumference.

A most significant characteristic of the ripe seed is its very hard outer coat (testa); to enable it to absorb water and thus germinate, the testa must be eroded either by natural wind-blasting on a sandy beach or by artificial scarification (using sandpaper or a sharp knife). This impermeable testa permits the seed to float in fresh and saline water for at least five years – ample time for trans-Atlantic dipersal, as the average drift time from west to east is about fifteen months.

When a seed is stranded on one of the beaches of western Ireland or Britain, it will not germinate immediately. The seed coat has to be eroded before water can be absorbed and in the meanwhile that seed may be buried or washed back out to sea. Even if the seed does germinate, the seedling still has to survive, for it too can be buried under wind-blown sand, swamped by salt water during Atlantic storms, trampled on by human beings, submerged under other more vigorous plants or eaten by slugs and snails. If it survives all this, flowering does not normally occur until three years after germination.

Thus, the chance of a seed developing into a mature plant on any Irish beach is small, and this is apparently confirmed by the species' infrequent appearance in Ireland. Over many years, plants were reported at Rossbeigh in County Kerry, and recently seedlings were spotted at Keel on Achill Island, County Mayo, and at Malinbeg in County Donegal. A report by Charles Smith in his *Civil and Natural History of the County of Kerry* (1756) of a white-flowered pea growing 'annually on the south point of Inch Island in the Bay of Castlemaine in considerable quantity' has been interpreted as the first record of the sea pea in Ireland, but it is more probably a record of an escaped garden pea, as *L. japonicus* does not have white flowers. The earliest authentic specimens were gathered by James Townsend Mackay on 'sandhills, Bay of Castlemaine' in 1804.

As far as the conservation of this species is concerned, it is illogical to include it in a list of endangered species, as the occasional, solitary Irish plants are indubitably mere immigrants, the fortuitous offspring of North American populations, flotsam of the wild Atlantic.

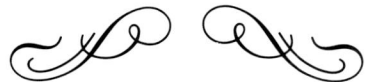

PLATE 4

Adiantum capillus-veneris Linnaeus

PLATE 4
Adiantum capillus-veneris Linnaeus

Adiantaceae							maidenhair fern, duchosach

This beautiful fern, with its characteristic fan-shaped leaf segments and black stems, is one of the species comprising the unique flora of the Burren in County Clare on the west coast of Ireland. Its typical habitat is the deep fissures (scailps or grykes) that criss-cross the bare limestone pavements; the maidenhair ferns are rooted in the peaty soil that accumulates at the bottom of the scailps and the fronds usually remain below the pavement surface.

Adiantum capillus-veneris is a cosmopolitan plant ranging throughout the tropics and subtropics but occasionally extending into temperate habitats, as in the coastal fringe of western Europe. In Ireland it is not restricted to the Burren, growing abundantly in similar habitats on the Aran Islands which lie offshore protecting the entrance to Galway Bay. Elsewhere it is rare, but it has been reported from counties Galway, Mayo, Sligo, Leitrim, Fermanagh and Donegal. In Britain it is almost confined to the southwest.

The maidenhair fern has a slender, creeping rhizome which is branched. From this arise the triangular fronds; in the mildest areas, the young fronds begin to emerge in early March. When fully developed, each frond may be as much as 60 cm tall, but more usually they are about 25 cm long. The fronds are erect or, when a plant is established on a vertical rock-face, they hang gracefully. The stipe (stalk) is shining black – hence the Irish name duchosach (black foot) – and slender, and smooth apart from a tuft of dark, pointed scales towards the base. The fan-shaped segments which compose the pinnae are translucent emerald-green when young, becoming duller and darker as they age. The shape of the frond segments is fairly constant, but their size and the degree to which the margins are lobed can vary considerably. Some of the segments may bear sori (these enclose the sporangia in which the spores are produced) near the margin on the lower surface. The fronds usually survive only until the autumn, but in very sheltered places in the mildest areas they may persist until the following year.

Edward Lhuyd, the Welsh antiquarian and naturalist who visited Ireland twice – his most important visit was in 1699 and 1700 – was the first to record the maidenhair fern from Ireland; he reported that 'in the isles of Aran near Galloway [*sic*] we find a great plenty'. The fern is not scarce on the Aran Islands nor in the Burren, but it would be intolerable today if the predation described by the Reverend John Keogh in 1735 should continue; he stated that *Adiantum* was brought to Dublin by the sackful for sale. And John Millington Synge recorded that he gathered the fern by the basketful on Inishmaan. Ancient tradition perhaps accounts for this; the maidenhair fern was credited with the cure of many ailments: according to John Gerard in his *Herball* of 1597, it 'expelleth... the stones in the kidneies... it raiseth up grosse and slimie humors out of the chest and lungs, and also those which sticke in the conduits of the winde pipe... it consumeth and wasteth away the Kings evill... and it maketh the haire of the head or beard to growe that is fallen and pilled off.' Gerard warned, however, that 'Whoso will followe the variable opinions of writers, concerning the Ferne called *Adianthum verum*, or *Capillus veneris verus*, must of necessitie be brought into a labyrinth of doubts, considering the divers opinions thereof...'.

4 Cultivated by Mrs W. F. Walsh, Lusk, County Dublin (from the Burren, County Clare), 15 August 1984. [×0.6]

PLATE 5

Saxifraga hirsuta Linnaeus,

S. *spathularis* Brotero and

S. ×*polita* (Haworth) Link

PLATE 5
Saxifraga hirsuta Linnaeus,
S. spathularis Brotero and
S. × polita (Haworth) Link

Saxifragaceae

kidney saxifrage, moran giobach
St Patrick's cabbage, cabaiste an mhadra rua

Saxifraga is a large genus containing about three hundred species which are distributed in arctic and temperate regions of Eurasia and North America, and on the higher parts of the Andes in South America. Eleven species are known in Ireland, ranging from the minute purple-flowered *S. oppositifolia* L. which grows on cool, shaded mountain ledges in the west and north, to the mossy saxifrages (for example *S. rosacea* Moench. and *S. hypnoides* L.) which are found, among other places, in the Burren.

The large-leaved saxifrages, commonly grouped together as the Robertsonian saxifrages (*Saxifraga* Sect. *Robertsoniana* (Haw.) Engl.), also occur in Ireland and are among the most interesting plants in the Irish flora. They are members of the Lusitanian element which also includes *Arbutus unedo* L. (AIF I: Plate 14), *Erica mackaiana* Bab. (AIF I: Plate 15), *E. erigena* R. Ross (Plate 11), *Daboecia cantabrica* (Huds.) Koch (AIF I: Plate 17), and *Pinguicula grandiflora* Lam. (AIF I: Plate 10); none of these plants occurs as native species in Britain but they do link the floras of Ireland and the Iberian Peninsula.

The occurrence in Ireland of these relatives of the London pride of gardens (*Saxifraga* × *urbium* D. A. Webb) has been known for almost three centuries. In 'A discourse concerning the large horns frequently found under ground in Ireland... with remarks on some other things natural to that country' published in the *Philosophical Transactions of the Royal Society* in 1696, Dr Thomas Molyneux reported that '*Cotyledon sive Sedum serratum Latifolium Montanum guttato flore* grows plentifully here with us in Ireland, on a Mountain call'd the Mangerton in Kerry, Six or Seven miles over... Two miles from the Town of Killarny... Here it spreads it self so abundantly, as to cover great parts of the Mountain.' The elaborate phrase in Latin describes the plant now named *Saxifraga spathularis*. Both that species and the kidney saxifrage were collected a few years later in 1700 by Edward Lhuyd (see also Plates 3 and 11) 'on the Mountains of Keri'.

In the nineteenth century, many variants of these saxifrages were collected by the numerous botanists who travelled to the west of Ireland. When they noticed a plant that differed from the archetypal form, they believed that they had discovered a new species and proceeded to name and describe it. Thus, by the end of the century there was a plethora of named 'species'. Reginald Scully (see Plate 6) and Professor Henry Dixon of Trinity College, Dublin, set about trying to discover the relationship between the variants and to test the hypothesis that some were hybrids. An experiment was set up in the College Botanic Garden, and artificial hybrids were raised from wild plants collected in Kerry. This led them to conclude that some of the described species were indeed hybrids and that the substantial variation observed in the wild was the result of interbreeding between the pure species and their own hybrids.

There remained, however, the problem of botanical nomenclature, and this was not satisfactorily resolved until Professor David Webb published the results of his studies in the middle of the present century. He established the valid names for the species: *S. hirsuta* (formerly *S. geum*) has small, round or kidney-shaped leaves with rounded teeth and long, terete pedicels; *S. spathularis* (formerly *S. umbrosa*) has obovate leaves the blades of which taper into a short, broad and flattened pedicel; *S.* × *polita* is the name for the hybrids.

Saxifraga hirsuta, the kidney saxifrage, is a rare plant found only in west County Cork and in County Kerry. It thrives in sheltered and shady places near streams, in rocky gullies and on mountain ledges as high as about 1000 m altitude. The flowers appear in the early summer, from May into July, and like those of the other species are white, occasionally with red markings. The five petals are about 0.5 cm long and elliptical. Each flower possesses ten stamens.

continued on page 36

5 *S. hirsuta* (centre): cultivated in Trinity College Botanic Garden, Dublin, 2 May 1985. *S. spathularis* (right) and *S.* × *polita* (left): cultivated by Dr E. C. Nelson, Celbridge, County Kildare, 26 May 1984 (both taxa originally from County Kerry). [×0.5]

continued

The plant known in Irish as cabaiste an mhadra rua (literally cabbage of the red dog, or fox's cabbage), and in Latin as *S. spathularis*, is much more widespread than the kidney saxifrage. It is recorded from counties Cork and Kerry in the southwest, from the Comeragh and Galtee mountains in counties Waterford and Tipperary, from Galway and Mayo in the west, from Wicklow and from Donegal in the northwest. The habitats in which *S. spathularis* grows resemble those favoured by *S. hirsuta* — shady places beside streams, in damp woodlands and on mountain rocks. It is locally abundant, spreading both vegetatively and by seed, and frequently cloaking boulders with its bright-green rosettes. Like the kidney saxifrage, fox's cabbage has white petals, about 0.5 cm long, marked with red spots. This saxifrage is sometimes called St Patrick's cabbage, an English name of doubtful, modern origin.

As the hybrid *S. × polita* is fertile, it can reproduce by seeds, and, like its parent species, it can also spread vegetatively by offsets which are produced prolifically. This ability easily to perpetuate itself explains why *S. × polita* exists in parts of Ireland — notably counties Galway and Mayo — where *S. hirsuta* has not been found since botanical recording began. In the distant past, it is suggested, the kidney saxifrage was more widespread than it is today, and grew in those two western counties. Hybrids were produced by cross-pollination with *S. spathularis* and the hybrids survived, but *S. hirsuta* (or both of the parent species) became extinct.

These saxifrages make attractive garden plants, and form excellent ground cover. They tolerate both acid and lime-rich soils, and may be propagated by offsets. More common is London pride, a mysterious plant which is a hybrid between *S. spathularis* and the true *S. umbrosa* L. This hybrid must have arisen in a garden many centuries ago, as it has never been found in the wild, although it is naturalized in Ireland and Britain, having escaped from gardens.

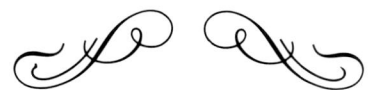

PLATE 6

Hieracium scullyi W. R. Linton

PLATE 6
Hieracium scullyi W. R. Linton

Asteraceae

Scully's hawkweed, lus na seabhac

Reginald William Scully (1858–1935), the original collector of this hawkweed, was the author of the *Flora of County Kerry* and co-editor with Nathaniel Colgan of the second edition of *Cybele Hibernica*. Dr Scully studied medicine but never practised as a doctor and spent much of his time botanizing. He lived in Rockfield House at Dundrum in the south of County Dublin for many years, and late in life moved to Rushbrooke near Cork.

Making Kerry his particular botanical parish, Reginald Scully tramped through most of that hilly county, and in the valley of the Roughty River, which enters the sea at Kenmare, he collected this hawkweed in 1894. It grows on the rocks in several places, at Morley's Bridge and at Drohidnagower Bridge, the population extending for about 3 km along the river valley. The hawkweed was recorded in the second edition of *Cybele Hibernica* as *Hieracium boreale* Fries. Scully sent specimens to the expert on these plants, the Reverend William R. Linton, vicar of Shirley, who decided that it represented a new species and named it in *An account of the British Hieracia* published in 1905.

I first encountered this plant in a Clonsilla garden, where it had been proudly planted but with a garbled name. Recognizing the true name, I was determined to see the plant in the wild and so visited the valley of the Roughty River in the summer of 1985. On the rocks by one of the bridges, and indeed on the stonework of the bridge itself, just as Scully has reported it, there were many plants of the same hawkweed. *H. scullyi* thus still flourishes in the spot where Reginald Scully found it, and it is not known to grow in any other part of Ireland or Britain.

Hieracium scullyi is a robust plant with stout, leafy stems reaching about 60 cm tall both in gardens and in the wild. The bright-green leaves are clothed beneath with hairs and with stiff marginal cilia. The basal rosette leaves are up to 10 cm long, oval and slightly toothed on the margins. The stem leaves, which number about ten, are ovate and clasp the stem. The dandelion-like flowers are relatively large for a hawkweed and there are two or three on each stem.

It is easy to cultivate. Although indigenous in a mild, sheltered valley, it is hardy and survived out-of-doors, without protection, in Celbridge during the cold winter of 1985–1986. It tolerates a heavy clay soil and blooms in July.

There are two other hawkweeds found only in Ireland: *H. hibernicum* F. J. Hanb. is confined to counties Donegal and Down, and *H. sparsifrons* P. D. Sell & C. West (= *H. sparsifolium* Lindeb. var. *oligodon* Linton) which is also restricted to the Roughty River in Kerry. All are microspecies, geographically isolated segregates of the variable group named *H. laevigatum* in *Flora Europaea*; in the context of Irish and British populations, the endemic microspecies are placed in Section *Tridentata*.

Reginald Scully is also commemorated in the hybrid between the Kerry butterwort, *Pinguicula grandiflora* Lam. (AIF I: Plate 10), and the common species, *P. vulgaris* L.; G. C. Druce named the progeny *Pinguicula × scullyi*.

6 Cultivated by Dr E. C. Nelson, Celbridge, County Kildare (from Roughty River, County Kerry, collected by Dr E. C. Nelson and Judy Cassells, June 1985), 11 July 1985. [×0.6]

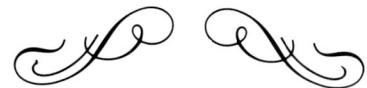

PLATE 7

Campanula rotundifolia Linnaeus

PLATE 7
Campanula rotundifolia Linnaeus

Campanulaceae   harebell, mearacan gorm

Campanula contains about three hundred species, most of which are inhabitants of temperate regions in the northern hemisphere. There are two species native in Ireland, one being the harebell, *Campanula rotundifolia*. The other, *C. trachelium* L., is only indigenous in County Offaly and along the Nore valley (counties Laois and Kilkenny); it has the delightful English name bats-in-the-belfry. Many other species and cultivars are grown in gardens and several of these cultivars have escaped and become naturalized. Also native in Ireland is the ivy-leaved bellflower which belongs to a different but related genus, *Wahlenbergia* (*W. hederacea* (L.) Reichb.).

Campanula rotundifolia grows throughout Ireland, but it tends to be more frequent in the west and north and is absent from some southeastern counties. It is a typical plant of stable coastal dunes and of dry grassy places on shallow soil, especially in basalt and limestone country. It also grows on rocky mountain slopes and ledges, ascending to over 1000 m altitude on the summit of Mount Brandon in County Kerry. The first record of *C. rotundifolia* in Ireland was published in Caleb Threlkeld's *Synopsis Stirpium Hibernicarum* (1726).

The harebell is a perennial with a slender, creeping, underground stolon from which rise the branched, flowering stems. The basal leaves vary in shape from oval to almost round; they have a cordate base and long, slender petiole. The leaves on the erect portion of the flowering stems are sessile and linear. The nodding blue bells are about 1.5 cm long and have five prominent lobes around the rim. Each stem bears several flowers, although occasional stems have just a single, terminal bell.

The harebell is a variable species and several varieties have been described and named. The most conspicuous variant is the white-flowered one, but this is extremely uncommon. Alexander More described *C. rotundifolia* var. *speciosa* based on specimens collected on Inishboffin, County Galway; he stated that it was a beautiful and distinct form, but it is not maintained as a distinct form today.

The harebell can be cultivated in gardens. It is lime-tolerant and may be raised from seed.

7 Lambay Island, County Dublin, collected by Mrs W. F. Walsh and Dr E. C. Nelson, 31 August 1985. [×0.75]

PLATE 8

Oxalis acetosella Linnaeus

PLATE 8
Oxalis acetosella Linnaeus

Oxalidaceae   wood sorrel, seamsog

'When this Plant has many Flowers, it presages Rains for that Year, and when it is thinly arrayed, it will be a dry Season: Dr Leonard Fuchsius... says, that this observation has been confirmed by frequent Experiments.'

So wrote the Reverend Caleb Threlkeld in 1726 in *Synopsis Stirpium Hibernicarum*, the first Irish flora. And it bloomed profusely in Celbridge in the spring of 1986, presaging the rains of that sodden summer!

The wood sorrel grows in Ireland's native woodlands, and it is especially tolerant of the dim light that penetrates to the forest floor. It also grows among rocks in sheltered nooks on mountain slopes, on shaded hedge-banks, and in the scailps criss-crossing the limestone pavements of the Burren. Wood sorrel requires plenty of moisture and flourishes in both acid and base-rich soils, so it can be cultivated easily in sheltered parts of the garden. Several colour forms are in cultivation, including a most elegant pink-flowered one.

The genus *Oxalis* contains more than eight hundred species which are especially abundant in Mexico, temperate and subtropical regions of South America, and in southern Africa. Some of the exotic species are cultivated in gardens, and a few of these having escaped from cultivation are now pernicious weeds – *O. corniculatus* L., which has small yellow flowers, is the principal one.

Oxalis acetosella is a widespread plant in the northern hemisphere, ranging through all the continents from Japan to Ireland, Iceland and eastern North America. It is a perennial herb with a creeping rhizome which has prominent swellings on it that act as storage organs. Adventitious roots arise from the rhizome. The grass-green leaves have long, erect stalks and three leaflets, each one more or less heart-shaped and about 1 cm long. In well-sheltered and mild areas the leaves may remain on the plant over winter.

The flowers appear in March and April, arising like the leaves from the rhizome on a slender, often red, peduncle which has two small bracts on the upper portion. The peduncles usually are longer than the leaf stalks, so the solitary flowers are held above the leaves. The flower is composed of an outer whorl of five greenish sepals about 0.3 cm long, and an inner whorl of translucent-white petals which are about 1.5 cm long; the petals are joined together towards the base and they have veins that sometimes are tinged with purple, and a yellow blotch at the base. There are ten stamens in two whorls of five. The ovary consists of five fused carpels, surmounted by five styles.

The reproductive biology of *O. acetosella* is complicated. Viable seeds are not produced by the spring flush of flowers. Most of the viable seeds are formed by flowers which appear in summer or early autumn and which are not usually visible but are concealed beneath the leaves. The seeds are expelled from the capsule when it ruptures explosively and they can be shot over one metre from the parent plant. This explosive discharge is most easily noticed in the weedy species such as *O. corniculatus* and is one of the reasons why that weed is so hard to control.

Wood sorrel has many vernacular names in English, including cuckoo's meat, Alleluia and stubwort. In Irish it is called seamsog, a word meaning worthless or trite. That name must not be confused with seamrog – shamrock.

Caleb Threlkeld, who was the first to publish the myth about St Patrick and the shamrock, did not equate the fictitious shamrock with *O. acetosella*; he followed other authors as far back as John Gerard who in 1597 ascribed the name shamrock to the red and white clovers, *Trifolium pratense* L. and *T. repens* L. respectively. Innumerable authors, most of whom should have known better, have used countless thousands of words attempting to prove that wood sorrel was the true and original shamrock held aloft by Ireland's patron saint while preaching a sermon on the Mystery of the Holy Trinity. As that story is a modern myth, any attempt to prove that wood sorrel, or indeed a clover, is the historical shamrock is utter folly.

In modern Ireland, immature plants of the clovers, especially of *T. dubium* L. (yellow clover), are worn as shamrock on 17 March, St Patrick's Day. Wood sorrel is never worn.

8 Celbridge, County Kildare, collected by Dr E. C. Nelson, 3 May 1986. [×0.9]

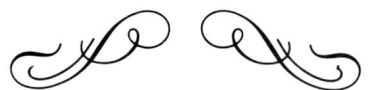

PLATE 9

Allium babingtonii Borrer

PLATE 9
Allium babingtonii Borrer

Alliaceae (Liliaceae)　　　　　　　　　　　　　　　　　　　　　　　　Babington's leek, cainneann

This graceful leek is perhaps one of the most ancient cultivated plants in Ireland but it is not now grown widely, indeed it is relatively uncommon in gardens. Yet the few gardeners who are nurturing it today are cultivating a plant that was most probably brought to Ireland about two thousand years ago from the Iberian Peninsula. Then it was grown as a pot-herb; today it is used mainly as an ornamental plant, although its culinary uses are not to be ignored.

Professor William Stearn's taxonomic studies of the European species of *Allium* led him to conclude that *A. babingtonii* represents the bulbilliferous state of the wide-ranging and variable *A. ampeloprasum* L. The name *A. babingtonii* coined by William Borrer in honour of Dr Charles Cardale Babington may be retained for this bulbil-bearing state.

Allium ampeloprasum has an interesting taxonomic history; it was originally named by Carl Linnaeus, who reported that it grew in the Orient and on Steep Holme Island in the Bristol Channel. Professor Stearn noted that this leek still grows on Steep Holme and suggests that the Steep Holme state can be 'reasonably accepted as representing the old cultivated stock of northern Europe'. *A. ampeloprasum* inhabits disturbed ground and cliffs throughout southern Europe, north Africa and western Asia; around the Mediterranean Sea it is indigenous, but it was probably introduced into western and northwestern Europe.

The bulbilliferous plant was discovered in the early nineteenth century in Cornwall and later in Ireland near Roundstone, County Galway, and on the Aran Islands. Dr Babington identified it as *A. halleri* G. Don. William Borrer regarded it as a new species and renamed it in 1846. Of this plant, Stearn comments: 'In floral structure and habit *A. babingtonii* agrees so closely with non-bulbilliferous *A. ampeloprasum* that its occurrence here [in Ireland] in isolation from the main area of *A. ampeloprasum* suggests strongly that it is a relict of ancient cultivation which has survived over the centuries through vegetative propagation by bulbils and possibly came originally to Ireland from the Iberian Peninsula.'

In cultivation, Babington's leek begins growing in February, producing grey leaves arranged alternately, their sheaths clasping the round stem. The bulb is flattened, round in cross-section and up to 6 cm in diameter when fully formed; it does not produce offsets. The keeled leaves extend to about 75 cm and are 3 to 4 cm broad with finely serrated margins. In late June the flowering spike begins to emerge; the stem is cylindrical and when fully extended is often over 2 m tall. At its tip is the cluster of bulbils and flowers which initially is enclosed in a spathe with a prolonged, flattened beak. The number of bulbils varies but at maturity the largest cluster may be about 10 cm across and will be composed of about fifty large bulbils and many more minute ones. Each flower – the number of flowers roughly equals the number of bulbils – is borne on a long slender pedicel; there are six pale-purple perianth segments and six stamens. Some of the pedicels are longer and bear secondary clusters of minute bulbils or flowers. Seeds are not formed, as the plant reproduces prolifically by bulbils.

It is hardy and grows well even in heavy clay soils. I leave the bulbs in the ground throughout the year; they are never lifted.

9 Cultivated by Dr E. C. Nelson, Celbridge, County Kildare (bulbils originally from Inishmore, Aran Islands); vegetative state: 15 February 1984; flowers: 16 July 1984. [×0.6]

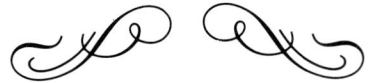

PLATE 10
Scilla verna Hudson

PLATE 10
Scilla verna Hudson

Liliaceae spring squill, sciolla earraigh

The Reverend Richard Heaton found *Hyacinthus stellarius vernus pumilus* (small spring starred hyacinth) 'at the Ring's End neere Dublin' sometime between 1633 and 1640. The discovery was published in 1650 by William How in his little flora *Phytologia Britannica*. Thus the spring squill was one of the first of Ireland's native plants recorded in a scientific manner.

Scilla verna is an interesting and beautiful member of the flora. It is found only in the east and north and is restricted to the coast. It grows in rocky places and on stable sand dunes where there is a mature grassy sward. The small, pear-shaped bulbs, about 2 cm long, are buried about 4 cm below the ground surface. Each bulb usually produces three dull-green leaves, which appear before the flowers; they are often curved and tend to lie horizontally on the ground. The largest leaves may be over 10 cm long and 0.5 cm broad. The solitary flowering stem emerges in the spring and may reach 10 cm in height, but usually it is shorter. At its tip there is a cluster of about ten star-shaped flowers on short (to 1.5 cm long) stalks, and with one conspicuous bluish bract, 1 to 1.5 cm long, attached at the base of each stalk. The six perianth segments are petal-like, pale blue tinged with purple, and are not fused. There are six stamens with blue filaments and dark anthers. The central ovary is dark blue.

The spring squill does not grow at Ringsend today – suburban developments obliterated it long ago – but it thrives in many places between Derry and Wexford. There is one perplexing record made by John Templeton (see Plate 1) who found a variant 'of a pale red at Ardglass – on the western side of Ardglass harbour and on the low ground near the head of the harbour'; such a colour-form has not been reported elsewhere, nor has it been seen at Ardglass, County Down, in modern times.

In Britain, *S. verna* is very local. It grows in Cornwall and Devon, and occurs along the west coast of Wales and Scotland, on the Hebrides, Orkney and Shetland, and on the northeastern coast northwards from Northumberland. On the European mainland it is restricted to the Iberian Peninsula, western France and Norway. There are also populations on the Faeroes.

This dwarf bulb can be grown in gardens, in deep, well-drained soil; it is an ideal plant for troughs and raised beds.

10 Clogher Head, County Louth, collected by Philip Shuttleworth and Mrs W. F. Walsh, 3 May 1984 (single flowering bulb and details, 13 May 1985). [×0.75]

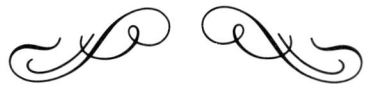

PLATE 11

Erica erigena R. Ross and

E. erigena f. *alba* (W. J. Bean) D. McClintock

PLATE 11

Erica erigena R. Ross and
E. erigena f. *alba* (W. J. Bean) D. McClintock

Ericaceae   Irish heather, fraoch camogach

Erica erigena is unique among the heathers growing wild in Ireland and Britain because it blooms in the late winter and spring; all the other species are summer-flowering shrubs. Indeed, it is one of a small group of plants which blossom early in the year – the most conspicuous shrub in flower with the Irish heather is gorse (*Ulex europaeus* L.; AIF I: Plate 18).

There are several characteristics of the Irish heather which distinguish it clearly from the other Irish species of *Erica*. Mature plants may be up to 3 m tall, especially if they are growing in sheltered habitats. They have erect, leafy branches, abundantly clothed in fine evergreen leaves, each one linear and about 0.5 cm long. The dark-green leaves are devoid of hairs and are arranged in whorls of four. The individual flowers have a tubular corolla about 0.5 cm long, from the mouth of which the anthers emerge.

In the wild there is little conspicuous variation in flower colour in this heather; pure-white flowers are extremely rare, but shrubs with very pale purple flowers are occasionally seen. The population in Connemara has generally paler flowers than plants from Mayo. In cultivation some excellent colour forms are known, including the beautiful pink variants which David McClintock gathered at Lough Carrowmore, County Mayo, in 1966 – these are in commerce as 'Irish Salmon' and 'Irish Dusk'.

Erica erigena was discovered in Ireland in 1700 by the Welsh naturalist Edward Lhuyd, who also was the first to find *Adiantum capillus-veneris* L. (Plate 4). However, he did not recognize the heather as it was not in flower, and his record remained unpublished. Over one century later, in 1830, James Mackay of the College Botanic Garden, Dublin, collected the Irish heather on Errisbeg Mountain at Roundstone in Connemara and the credit for the 'discovery' of this plant was generally given to him. In subsequent years the heather was traced from Errisbeg northwards into Mayo as far as the Mullet Peninsula. It is said that the Irish populations of *E. erigena* are the most extensive in western Europe, but the species is not uncommon in its Iberian sites.

E. erigena is not native in Britain and the nearest population on the European mainland is near Bordeaux on the west coast of France. The heather also grows in widely scattered localities in Spain and Portugal. Its disrupted (disjunct) distribution pattern reflects those of several other members of the Ericaceae which are native in Ireland, including *E. mackaiana* Bab. (AIF I: Plate 15), *Arbutus unedo* L. (AIF I: Plate 14) and *Daboecia cantabrica* (Huds.) Koch (AIF I: Plate 17). However, its distribution pattern shows some significant differences which have led Professor Webb to comment that the distribution of *E. erigena* cannot be explained by the standard theories applied to disjunctions in the European flora. Perhaps it has, according to Professor Webb, some 'quite unexplained power of long-distance dispersal, or else it underwent a severe fragmentation of area some time ago'. Another possibility is that it is expanding its range; in Ireland, at least, *E. erigena* is an opportunist, colonizing old railway embankments, cut-over bogs, and even lough shores laid bare when water levels are lowered as at Lough Carrowmore in County Mayo. One of its most remarkable colonies grows on the lazy beds of the derelict clachan on the southern slope of Mweelrea by the shore of Killary Harbour. Thus, it is not confined to pristine moorlands and unaltered mountainsides. Man's activities certainly assist its spread.

The ecology of this fascinating plant, its phytosociology and its history in Ireland since the last glaciation have been studied by Dr Peter Foss, University College, Dublin. Detailed distribution maps for the plant in Ireland have also been prepared recently by Dr Foss, Dr Gerry Doyle and Dr Charles Nelson.

Like so many plants, the Irish heath has had a bewildering number of botanical names. Originally it was named *Erica mediterranea* auct. non L., and when this was found to be invalid, it was called *E. hibernica* (Hook. & Arn.) Syme, a name which was also discovered to be illegit-

continued on page 60

11 Lough Furnace, County Mayo, collected by Dr E. C. Nelson, 11 April 1984. White-flowered inset: cultivated in National Botanic Gardens, Glasnevin, 26 April 1985. [×0.7]

continued

imate. In 1966, Robert Ross published the name *E. erigena* for it, basing the specific epithet on a Latin name signifying a native of Eriu (an ancient name for Ireland); the Christian philosopher Johannes Scotus Eriugena is the most celebrated bearer of this name.

Erica erigena is closely allied to *E. carnea* L. (= *E. herbacea* L.); indeed, the only morphological difference is that the latter species is a prostrate, sprawling shrub. The distinctive habits are reflected in anatomical differences, but these do not serve as useful characters for separating herbarium or even fresh specimens. The prostrate habit of *E. carnea* is an adaptation to its habitats on the mountains of central southern Europe, where plants are frequently buried under deep winter snow; it is significant that heavy snow will easily shatter the branches of *E. erigena*. When grown together in gardens, these two species readily hybridize and fertile progeny (*E. ×darleyensis* W. J. Bean) is produced; hybrids are never produced in the wild, as the plants do not grow in adjacent habitats. When these features are carefully considered, it can be argued that the Irish heath is merely an erect, geographic variant of *E. carnea*, adapted for milder, snow-free habitats, and that it should be designated as a subspecies (*E. carnea* ssp. *occidentalis* (Benth.) Lainz).

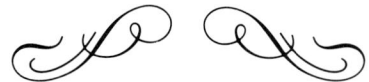

PLATE 12

Fuchsia magellanica Lamarck

PLATE 12
Fuchsia magellanica Lamarck

Onagraceae fiuise, singirlini, sugarlini

The hedges of western Ireland are spectacular in summer, dripping with the crimson and purple blossoms of *Fuchsia magellanica*, but this lovely shrub is not a native plant; it is an alien deliberately introduced by gardeners. All the same, it flourishes in the mild, moist climate of this island and is now as much a part of the Irish landscape as gorse and heather.

The home of *F. magellanica* is temperate South America, mainly southern Chile and Tierra del Fuego. The genus is composed of about one hundred species, the majority of which are from South and Central America. There is also one native in Tahiti, and several species are endemic in New Zealand. *Fuchsia* belongs to the same family as *Clarkia* (including *Godetia*), willow-herbs (*Epilobium* spp.), evening primroses (*Oenothera* spp.) and enchanter's night-shade (*Circaea lutetiana* L.).

Shrubs of *F. magellanica* reach over 3 m in height in mild areas where the shoots are not killed by winter frosts. Even in such areas, however, during cold winters the shrubs can be completely defoliated, leaving bare, cinnamon-coloured twigs; in mild winters and sheltered places the leaves may be retained. The leaves are ovate with toothed and slightly undulating margins; they are about 4 cm long with a short stalk. The solitary flowers produced at the stem nodes dangle on peduncles about 5 cm long. The outer whorl of each flower is formed from four bright-red sepals; these are about 2 cm long, tapering towards the tip. The inner purple whorl is composed of the petals, which are heart-shaped and up to 1 cm long. Emerging from the flower are eight long stamens, and a single, even longer, style.

The flowers secrete a copious supply of nectar which, in the plant's South American habitats, attracts hummingbirds to feed. The birds hover beside the flowers and probe their long bills into them. The hummingbirds' heads are dusted with pollen from the emergent anthers and so the birds act as pollinators. In Ireland, hummingbirds are absent, but honey bees and other nectar-seeking insects visit the flowers, and pollination does take place. The wind may also waft pollen from anther to stigma. After pollination, black, juicy berries are formed and these contain viable seeds. However, seedlings are rarely seen in the wild or in gardens in Ireland, probably because they are killed by the cold winter weather; seedlings have been raised in the National Botanic Gardens, Dublin, in heated glasshouses from fruits collected in County Clare, and Professor D. A. Webb has reported seedlings from the Aran Islands.

Under natural conditions in Ireland, *F. magellanica* does not spread rapidly: indeed, it is doubtful if it spreads at all without aid from man, as it does not produce far-ranging suckers. In one garden at least, at Glanleam on Valentia Island, it is recorded that a single shrub planted in 1854 increased to form a thicket almost 40 m (120 ft) in circumference by about 1872. This was achieved because the branches were allowed to layer naturally. In hedges this does not happen and the shrubs stay very much within bounds.

The history of *F. magellanica* in Ireland is poorly documented; indeed, its history in Europe is also somewhat mysterious. It is reported that the first plant reached England from Chile in 1788 and was donated by Captain Firth to the Royal Garden at Kew. Pressed specimens of this original introduction are extant and some authorities have identified them as a Brazilian species named *F. coccinea* Solander. But an illustration of this same plant appeared in 1789 in William Curtis's *Botanical Magazine*, and this suggests that the plant was *F. magellanica*. Confirmation that the Chilean plant was introduced apparently comes from cultivation records; *F. coccinea* is not hardy and could not survive out-of-doors in Europe, but as early as 23 November 1799, John Templeton reported that he had grown *Fuchsia* in the open without protection at Belfast: 'The Buddlea globosa and Fuchsia coccinea are other instances of plants, that without knowledge of their native climate, Chili, we would not suppose capable of being naturalized to ours. Yet is the Buddlea seldom injured by our cold, and the Fuchsia, although killed to the ground by the winter's cold, sends forth abundance of shoots which attain the height

continued on page 64

continued

of three feet in summer, and are decorated with its elegant flowers, which are larger and much more brilliant than ever they are when confined in a house.'

While John Templeton had *F. magellanica* in his garden in the 1790s, it was probably not widely distributed to other gardens until the first quarter of the nineteenth century. By the middle of the century, *F. magellanica* was well established, in western Ireland at least, as a garden plant. The Reverend W. M. Hind reported in 1857 that 'the common Fuchsia . . . attains to the size of a large shrub of fifteen feet or upwards' at Dingle. In the 1870s the first reports of hedges appear; one writer in *The Garden* on 5 October 1872 noted that 'the old Fuchsia is planted as an undergrowth, and forms dense masses, dripping with a crimson rain of drooping flowers . . . above the picturesque harbour of Glandore . . . I noticed several hedges of considerable extent formed entirely of Fuchsias, just then in the full glory of their bloom, and will it be believed? a ruthless wretch was shearing the hedge to make it thicker . . .'.

There are two distinct variants of *F. magellanica* used in Ireland for hedging. One, with buds which are about as broad as long, is most probably the cultivar 'Riccartonii' – this is the variant illustrated here. 'Riccartonii' was recorded by The Knight of Kerry in his garden at Glanleam, Valentia Island, County Kerry, and that is the plant still growing there. The other variant has slim buds, and approaches more closely the wild type; it is much rarer in hedges, and has been reported in various sources as "*Fuchsia gracilis*", an appropriate but invalid name. The difference in bud form is due to the difference in the maximum width of the sepals; in 'Riccartonii' the sepals are about 0.7 cm broad, whereas in "*F. gracilis*" they are only 0.4 cm across. It is not appropriate to subdivide the populations further, although occasional differences in the colour of foliage have been noticed; it is indeed probable that several cultivars of obscure origin were used last century as a source of hedge-plants.

Fuchsia was named in honour of the sixteenth-century German herbalist and botanist Leonhard Fuchs. The generic name is sometimes misspelt due to the inappropriate pronounciation that has been visited on the name; *Fuchsia* should be pronounced fuks-ee-a. The incorrectly pronounced name is, sadly, perpetuated in a newly devised Irish word – fiuise.

On the Dingle Peninsula this now ubiquitous interloper is called singirlini, 'the sound of which suggests the pendant flowers', and sugarlini, which is 'a deliberate bilingual hybrid coined by a bilingual people with a sense of humour'.

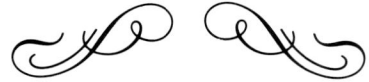

PLATE 13
Sisyrinchium angustifolium Miller

(syn. *S. bermudiana* auct. non L.; *S. hibernicum* A. & D. Löve)

PLATE 13
Sisyrinchium angustifolium Miller
(syn. *S. bermudiana* auct. non L.; *S. hibernicum* A. & D. Löve)

Iridaceae   blue-eyed grass, feilistrín gorm

Sisyrinchium is primarily an American genus; only one of the estimated seventy-five species occurs naturally outside the Americas, and that is our subject.

The botanical name of the Irish blue-eyed grass has been changed several times, much to the bewilderment of botanists, both amateur and professional. For many years it was known as *S. bermudiana* L., a name which is now fixed only on a larger-flowered, and thus more ornamental, species that is confined to Bermuda. The name *S. graminoides* Bicknell has also been employed, but it is merely a synonym of *S. angustifolium* which has been the name most generally attached to it.

Some authors believe that the Irish populations of the blue-eyed grass represent a distinct, endemic European species, and the name *S. hibernicum* was proposed by Askel and Doris Löve, but no Irish botanists have accepted this binomial and it does not appear in current European floras. The plant depicted in the illustration was collected at the Clonee Loughs, southwest of Kenmare in County Kerry, the type locality for *S. hibernicum*.

The problem of nomenclature is intimately linked with the morphology and cytology of the blue-eyed grass throughout its range. There are no clearly marked discontinuities in the morphology of some populations, although there are many perplexing differences in the numbers of chromosomes in the plants making up those populations. For example, Irish plants closely resemble some which occur in the eastern United States and Canada, but the populations have different diploid chromosome numbers (2n); in Irish populations 2n = 88 has been reported, in American and Canadian populations 2n = 32, 64, 80, 82, 84, 88, 90 or 96. Faced with this extraordinary variation in the invisible chromosomes, yet with no conspicuous morphological differences to separate the genetic types, there is plenty of room for arguments between taxonomists, and thus for a marvellous confusion of names.

To compound the problem as far as Irish plants are concerned, there is always the possibility that the blue-eyed grass was introduced from America into Ireland, and that it is not a true native species. It was discovered in 1845 by James Lynam, a civil engineer, at Woodford in the southeastern corner of County Galway. In 1882 blue-eyed grass was found in County Kerry, where it is now known to be relatively abundant. Plants were subsequently reported from counties Cork, Clare, Tipperary, Sligo, Leitrim, Fermanagh and Donegal, with a further record of doubtful status in Antrim. Most botanists agree that the blue-flowered species of *Sisyrinchium* found in Britain is an alien and that it is the same plant as that native in Ireland, but recently it has been suggested that it is not the same as the Irish blue-eyed grass. Further confusion reigns on the continent of Europe, where several species are reported as naturalized.

Sisyrinchium angustifolium is a herbaceous perennial. The leaves are grass-like, up to 20 cm long and about 0.3 cm broad; they are linear, sword-shaped and are grouped in a fan. The flowers are borne on an erect stem that may reach 50 cm in height and is distinctly flattened with narrow wings. Each flower-spike bears two or more stalked blossoms. There are six petal-like perianth segments, each about 0.6 cm long, with a distinct point at the tip; the inner surface is bright blue, and the outer is a pale greyish-blue. The filaments of the six stamens are fused together and surround the capsule, which bears a three-lobed stigma. The capsule darkens as it becomes ripe and usually contains several black, shining seeds.

The blue-eyed grass inhabits damp meadows, the shores of loughs and river banks. While relatively abundant in the Republic of Ireland, where it is not protected by law, it is included in the list of species covered by conservation legislation in Northern Ireland (Wildlife (Northern Ireland) Order 1985, schedule 8, pt 1). It may be cultivated in gardens and does not require a boggy situation; good garden loam suffices. Blue-eyed grass can be raised from seeds, and established clumps may be divided.

13 Clonee Loughs, County Kerry, collected by Dr E. C. Nelson and Judy Cassells, 20 June 1985. [×0.65]

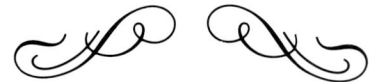

PLATE 14
Trollius europaeus Linnaeus

PLATE 14
Trollius europaeus Linnaeus

Ranunculaceae

globe flower, leolach

The genus *Trollius*, which is closely related to the buttercups (*Ranunculus*), includes about twelve species that inhabit arctic and temperate areas of North America, Europe and Asia. Only one of these, *Trollius europaeus*, occurs as a native plant in Ireland, although several of the Asian species and their horticultural hybrids are grown in gardens.

Trollius europaeus is restricted to a few habitats in northwestern Ireland, to counties Fermanagh and Donegal. In Britain it is much more widespread, growing beside lakes and in damp meadows and woodlands from South Wales northwards into Scotland, where it occurs on mountains at altitudes up to about 1200 m. The same species ranges throughout Europe, extending as far north as Arctic Norway, eastwards into the Caucasus, and also in Arctic areas of North America.

The Irish populations of the globe flower are fully protected by laws in Northern Ireland and in the Republic of Ireland. In County Fermanagh, this plant is recorded on the eastern shore of Lough Melvin – it has been known from Gorminish Island for over eighty years but has recently spread to Rosskit – and on the northern shore of Upper Lough Macnean a few kilometres west of Belcoo, a site not formally reported in botanical literature. The plants inhabit a very narrow strip about the high-water mark in the fringing alder woodland. In County Donegal, globe flowers grow on the shores of Lough Gartan, and there are records of plants in the valley of the River Finn, but the globe flower is not found there today.

Trollius europaeus is a deciduous herb with a perennial rootstock. The stalked leaves appear in spring; they are glabrous, pentagonal in outline but lobed and the lobes are also toothed and cut. The flowers are borne on tall, leafy stems which may be as much as 75 cm high; each stem bears a solitary (very occasionally two or three) terminal bud. The characteristic blossom is about 3 cm in diameter, globe-shaped, composed of about ten concave sepals which are yellow and petal-like; the true petals are the small, yellow nectaries which are concealed within the globe of sepals. There are numerous stamens. The carpels in the centre of each flower are not fused together; they contain two rows of ovules which, after pollination, develop into shining black seeds. Globe flowers are pollinated by insects and they bloom in late May and June.

The European globe flower has been cultivated for at least four centuries in British gardens – Charles de l'Ecluse (Clusius) saw it in London in 1581 and it is mentioned by John Gerard in his great *Herball* of 1597. An easy plant to grow, it thrives in moist, rich loam and tolerates lime, and makes an attractive subject for herbaceous or mixed borders. About the beginning of this century, the Daisy Hill Nursery, Newry, County Down, raised a series of orange-flowered cultivars, including 'Orangeman' and 'Prince of Orange' – their lineage will have included *T. asiaticus* L.

14 Cultivated by Mrs Moody, Rosskit, Garrison, County Fermanagh (from indigenous population), 1 June 1985. [×0.6]

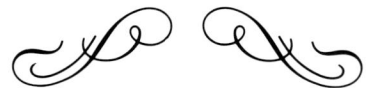

PLATE 15

Anemone nemorosa Linnaeus

'Lady Doneraile' and 'Lucy's Wood'

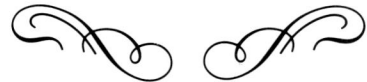

PLATE 15

Anemone nemorosa Linnaeus
'Lady Doneraile' and 'Lucy's Wood'

Ranunculaceae								wood anemone, lus na gaoithe

The buttercup family, Ranunculaceae, comprises about fifty genera and 1300 species; such diverse garden plants as *Clematis*, *Trollius*, *Anemone*, *Aconitum*, *Delphinium*, *Aquilegia*, *Helleborus* and *Thalictrum* belong to the family. Among Ireland's native flora, Ranunculaceae is represented by the buttercups and crowfoots (*Ranunculus* spp.), marsh marigold (*Caltha palustris* L.), columbine (*Aquilegia vulgaris* L.), the rues (*Thalictrum* spp.), globe flower (*Trollius europaeus*, see Plate 14) and the wood anemone.

So characteristic of springtime, wood anemones form one of the major components of the flora of the wild woods, but they often survive in open ground, indicating that long ago a forest had grown there. In the Burren, County Clare, wood anemones grow in the hazel scrub and out on the pavement among the limestone rocks with other woodland plants, including the primrose (Plate 16).

Anemone nemorosa is a perennial herb with a creeping, underground rhizome which is branched and forms a network in the woodland soil. From the rhizome arises the flowering stem. This simply consists of an erect stalk with a ruff of three leaves about the mid-point; above the leaves stands a solitary flower. The stem leaves are palmately divided and toothed; the degree of lobing varies from plant to plant and some leaves may be very deeply and finely cut so that the ruff is fern-like. The flower is composed usually of a whorl of five to seven white, petal-like perianth segments – the number varies and some plants may have as many as ten segments. Inside this whorl are numerous stamens; again the number varies but the average is about sixty. All of the stamens are fertile and there are no nectaries in this species. The centre of the flower is composed of a cluster of green carpels.

The variability of *A. nemorosa* has been exploited by gardeners who have selected some of the best or most interesting forms for cultivation. As wood anemones can be increased easily by vegetative propagation, by dividing the network of rhizomes, some of the variants are now widely grown.

A beautiful blue-flowered cultivar named 'Robinsoniana' was in gardens in the latter half of the last century; the outer side of the perianth is fawn and the inner a delicate lavender-blue. It was said to have originated in Ireland, and was given prominence by William Robinson, the Irish-born gardener and author of *The English Flower Garden*, from whom it takes its name.

The blue-flowered variant in our plate is indubitably Irish, having been found in Lucy's Wood, a small copse near the town of Bunclody, County Wexford, by Evelyn Booth. She brought it into her own garden – her house also bears the name Lucy's Wood – where it proliferated rapidly. It is a distinct clone, not related to 'Robinsoniana'. The flowers are large, 4.5 cm across, with six or seven broad (2.5 cm long, 1.2 cm wide) perianth segments which inside are bright blue slightly tinged with violet; the outside of the segments is a shade paler. The rhizome is thick and stout, about 0.5 cm in diameter, and the stems are sparsely hirsute.

The white-flowered wood anemone is another Irish clone named 'Lady Doneraile'. E. A. Bowles stated that it was found in Ireland about the turn of the century by Viscountess Doneraile. In 1984, in a derelict garden near Doneraile, County Cork, Megan Morris found wood anemones closely resembling this one. It is a robust plant, reaching about 25 cm in height, and bearing large, white flowers which may be over 4.5 cm in diameter. The Very Reverend Ulrich Toubol, Dean of Maribo Cathedral in Denmark, described this cultivar as a 'wonderful anemone. The flowers when open face upwards so that they resemble miniature sunflowers.'

There are other Irish cultivars of *A. nemorosa*. Miss Fanny Currey of Lismore, County Waterford, who is best remembered as daffodil breeder, sent E. A. Bowles pink and blue forms from the woods at Lismore. These are still in cultivation as 'Lismore Blue' and 'Lismore Pink' (a plant mentioned by Ulrich Toubol as 'Currie's Pink' is perhaps this too). Dr Molly Sanderson has made a good collection of wood anemones and two from her garden (but originally from

continued on page 76

15 'Lucy's Wood' (left) cultivated by Miss Evelyn Booth, Bunclody, County Wexford, 11 May 1986. 'Lady Doneraile' (centre and right) cultivated by Dr E. C. Nelson, Celbridge, County Kildare (from Dr Molly Sanderson), 21 April 1986. [×0.6]

continued

Scandinavia) have been named 'Green Fingers' and 'Green Dream'. Ulrich Toubol also mentions a blue-flowered wood anemone with infolded leaves; its most striking characteristic is the bright-red bud. He quoted the name 'Hannah Gubbay' for it, but this may be a corruption of 'Robinsoniana Cornubiense', a red-budded plant which was listed by Daisy Hill Nursery, Newry, early this century.

Wood anemones require no special treatment in gardens. They thrive in clay soils and lime-rich loam. The cultivars should be propagated by division of the rhizomes.

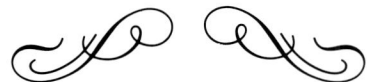

PLATE 16

Primula vulgaris Linnaeus and

P. vulgaris 'Elizabeth Dickey'

PLATE 16
Primula vulgaris Linnaeus and
P. vulgaris 'Elizabeth Dickey'

Primulaceae   primrose, bainne bó bleacht

Ireland has only two native species of *Primula*, the cowslip (*P. veris* L.; AIF I: Plate 13) and the primrose. Cowslips have declined in abundance so much that they are now fully protected in Northern Ireland. However, in parts of western Ireland, especially on stable sand dunes and rough, lime-rich pastures, the cowslip is still frequent and it is not listed among the protected species in the Republic of Ireland. Happily, primroses are common in woodlands, on hedgebanks and coastal dunes. They do not require protection yet. But, as in the case of cowslips, over-picking could cause a rapid decline in the numbers of primroses.

Primula vulgaris is a perennial, tufted herb with spathulate leaves up to 15 cm long and about 7 cm broad. Each leaf has a prominent mid-rib and a wrinkled surface. The flowers appear in late winter and early spring – in a mild year primroses may be seen blooming in January, especially in southern and western areas. Each pale-yellow flower is held on a slender, hairy stalk, but occasionally plants may be found which have clustered flowers; these are the so-called 'polyanthus' forms.

The primrose has a deceptively complicated flower. Some plants have a style which is longer than the stamens, so that the stigma emerges from the flower – the flower looks as if it has a small, yellow pin emerging from the throat and these plants are appropriately dubbed 'pin-eyed'. A second form has a short style, so that the stigma is concealed by the stamens which appear at the throat – this form is called 'thrum'. To set seed, pollen from a 'thrum' primrose must be transferred to the stigma of a 'pin-eyed' plant, or pollen from a 'pin-eyed' to the stigma of a 'thrum'. 'Pin-eyed' and 'thrum' primroses are equally common, and most populations contain both types.

Very infrequently, unusual mutants are discovered in the wild. Primroses with pure-white flowers have been reported from Ireland, as have plants with red blossoms. 'Jack-in-the-green' and 'hose-in-hose' primroses also occur, and at least one double-flowered primrose has been collected in Ireland. The double-flowered form actually has multipetalled flowers in which all the sexual organs (pistil and stamens) have been replaced by petals. These plants are sterile and can never set seed, although they may produce an occasional stamen and thus pollen.

The double-flowered cultivar 'Elizabeth Dickey' came from Ballymoney in County Antrim. Like many of the older cultivars of primrose, it is not readily available from nurseries nor is it abundant in gardens, but it has been kept alive for about fifty years by gardeners who live around Ballymoney.

A young girl, Elizabeth Dickey, was out for a walk one day and gathered some primroses from the local hedge-banks. She brought the posy home and gave it to her mother, who noticed that one of the flowers was double. Elizabeth retraced her steps and eventually found the plant, which her mother carefully transplanted. For many years mother and daughter kept this lovely double-flowered form in their own gardens and eventually Dr Molly Sanderson obtained an offshoot. Dr Sanderson in turn gave offshoots to David Chalmers of Stonehaven, a nurseryman specializing in the older cultivars of primrose, and she suggested that the cultivar should be named after both the little girl who had found it and her mother.

Primula vulgaris 'Elizabeth Dickey' was introduced into commerce by Chalmers in the 1970s and is sometimes offered by primrose nurseries. It must be propagated by division. The wild primrose can be raised easily by sowing fresh seed; several firms now sell seeds of native plants so that the gathering of seeds from the wild is not necessary. Once established, plants may also be propagated by dividing them; the best time is immediately after flowering or in the autumn.

16 *P. vulgaris*: Lusk, County Dublin, collected by Mrs W. F. Walsh, 27 April 1984. 'Elizabeth Dickey' (top): cultivated by Mrs W. F. Walsh, Lusk, County Dublin (from Dr Molly Sanderson), 15 May 1986. [×0.6]

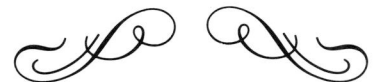

PLATE 17

Primula edgeworthii (J. D. Hooker) Pax

PLATE 17
Primula edgeworthii (J. D. Hooker) Pax

Primulaceae   Edgeworth's primrose

Of the few plants that bloom out-of-doors during an Irish winter, this primrose is undoubtedly one of the most beautiful. It begins to blossom in January and continues bearing flowers until March; but it is not easy to cultivate. By chance, I have succeeded in providing it with a congenial spot, on a raised peat bed, facing north so that it never gets sun except for a few brief hours in mid-summer. An occasional liquid feed is given in summer and a liberal dressing of whatever will keep vine weevils at bay. In the first winter I did not cover the plants, leaving them open to the rain and snow, but they did not flower well. During their second winter, from the end of November the plants were covered with a simple sheet of glass so that they did not get wet, but there was free movement of air. The plants blossomed profusely and never suffered, even during the coldest and driest periods; they were never given water.

Primula edgeworthii is one of the "Petiolarids" primroses (*Primula* sect. *Petiolares*), a group of species from the Himalaya which also includes *P. petiolaris* Wallich, *P. gracilipes* Craib, *P. bhutanica* Fletcher, *P. whitei* W. W. Sm. and *P. sonchifolia* Franch. They generally form winter-resting buds with small leaves, and in summer they develop much larger leaves. This seasonal dimorphism has led to a plethora of names being applied to the species now called *Primula edgeworthii*.

In its winter state, the leaves are formed tightly into a rosette with the developing flower-buds clearly visible in the centre and everything is covered in a golden-white, floury meal, especially if protected by glass; the winter leaves (3 to 4 cm long) are spathulate with short, winged petioles and toothed margins. The summer leaves are larger, up to 15 cm long and as much as 6 cm broad; they are broadly ovate on long, slender stalks and, like the winter leaves, have marginal teeth, but they are not as densely covered in white meal. The flowers are borne on stalks about 6 cm long and the bud and stalk are covered in the same white meal as the leaves. The corolla has a yellow throat and five spreading lobes, which are mauve fading to white in the centre; the lobes are irregularly but clearly toothed.

This exquisite primrose comes from woods and hill-slopes in the Himalaya between 2000 and 4000 m altitude. Roland Cooper described it growing 'in the shade of the Birch and Spruce forest, usually by moist stream edges'. Its roots grow deep into the peaty soil as these streams dry up in winter when the cold traps the water in ice and snow on the high peaks.

The first person to collect this primrose was Richard Blinkworth; he gathered the spring stage in Kumaon about 1824. His friend, the botanist Nathanial Wallich of Calcutta Botanic Garden, thought the plant was the same as one he had named *P. petiolaris*. About twenty years later, Edward Madden (see Plate 18) found this primrose in the valley below the Pindari Glacier, and he gave specimens to Michael Pakenham Edgeworth, who decided it was a new species and proposed (but never published) the name "Primula pulverulenta" for it. About the same time, Edgeworth himself gathered specimens by the River Alaknanda, but he did not connect the different seasonal forms of the primrose. Other collectors added specimens to the pool of material and in 1882 Joseph Hooker realized that all these gatherings represented just one species, but he made the mistake of separating the winter and summer states into two distinct botanical varieties: *P. petiolaris* var. *pulverulenta* for the winter one, and *P. petiolaris* var. *edgeworthii* for the summer state. When at last it was realized that these were simply dimorphic seasonal states of one species, the earliest, precisely attributable name available for the primrose was *P. edgworthii*.

Michael Pakenham Edgeworth (1812–1881), born at the family home in Edgeworthstown, County Longford, was a distinguished botanist in his own right. He wrote a treatise on pollen and he was a friend of Edward Madden and of Joseph Hooker. His contribution to the task of introducing Himalayan plants into cultivation in Europe has not been fully explored, and while he is not known to have gathered seeds of this primrose, he did send seeds of other plants,

continued on page 84

17 Cultivated by Dr E. C. Nelson, Celbridge, County Kildare, 8 February 1986. [×0.8]

continued

including *Buddleja crispa* Benth. (see Plate 18), to his half-sister, Maria.

He is commemorated in a number of different plants, and the genus *Edgeworthia* was dedicated to him by Karl Meissner.

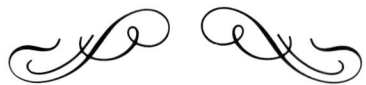

PLATE 18

Buddleja crispa Bentham

PLATE 18
Buddleja crispa Bentham

Loganiaceae · butterfly bush

The family name Loganiaceae is derived from the type genus *Logania* from Australasia, which was named by Robert Brown in honour of the Irish-born American naturalist James Logan (1674–1751). A native of Lurgan who journeyed to America in 1699 with William Penn, Logan settled near Philadelphia and became 'the most important and most influential public figure in ... Pennsylvania during the first half of the eighteenth century'. He was also a keen naturalist and book-collector, and conducted a considerable correspondence with scientists, including fellow-Ulsterman Sir Hans Sloane. Logan wrote *Experimenta et meletemata de plantarum generatione*, one of the earliest discussions on sexual reproduction in plants; this was published at Leiden in 1739 and London in 1747.

Buddleja was named by Carl Linnaeus in memory of a contemporary of James Logan, the Reverend Adam Buddle, rector of Gray's Inn, London, who died in 1715; he was an amateur botanist with an interest in mosses and grasses. The preferred spelling of the Latin name is *Buddleja* (which is the form used by Linnaeus) rather than *Buddleia*.

Buddleja is a large genus of over one hundred species. Most of these are native in eastern Asia, but there are also representatives in South America – the best known being the orange ball tree (*B. globosa* Hope) – and in southern Africa. The most widely cultivated species are those from Asia, and the butterfly bush (*B. davidii* Franch.) is now familiar as a weedy shrub on derelict building lots in towns and cities. There are some cultivars of Irish origin, including the enigmatic *B. davidii* 'Glasnevin Blue' and the Howth and Rowallane variants of *B. colvilei* Hook. f. & Thoms. *B. crispa*, one of the Asian species, is not a common plant in Irish gardens, although it first flowered here over a century ago.

For many years, Edward Madden has been credited with the introduction of *B. crispa* into cultivation in Europe. He sent seeds to David Moore, curator of the Royal Dublin Society's Botanic Gardens, Glasnevin, where it was grown under glass and flowered for the first time in 1854. Major Madden introduced a number of fine plants through Glasnevin, including the highly scented shrub *Abelia triflora* R. Br. (AIF I: Plate 41) and the giant Himalayan lily *Cardiocrinum giganteum* (Wall.) Makino. But recent research among the papers of Michael Pakenham Edgeworth has revealed a list of seeds which he sent to his half-sister, the novelist Maria Edgeworth, in June 1841; *B. crispa* is listed but there is no additional information given, so it is not known if Miss Edgeworth succeeded in raising seedlings from any of her brother's seeds. If in her garden at Edgeworthstown, County Longford, she did raise young plants of *B. crispa*, they would have predated Major Madden's introductions by about ten years.

Michael Pakenham Edgeworth was the son of Richard Lowell Edgeworth and his fourth wife Frances Beaufort; Maria was Richard's eldest child by his first wife Anna Elers. Pakenham Edgeworth knew Edward Madden well, as they both lived and worked in India during the 1830s and 1840s. Edgeworth even acted as courier for Madden on at least one occasion, personally delivering Himalayan seeds to Glasnevin in 1846. Frequently, the same plant species were collected by Madden and Edgeworth during their separate travels in the Himalaya; apart from *B. crispa*, there are specimens of *Primula edgeworthii* Pax (see Plate 17) gathered by Madden and by Edgeworth.

Buddleja crispa is a variable species – plants grown as *B. farreri* Balf. f. & W. W. Sm. (with large, felted leaves) and as *B. caryopteridifolia* W. W. Sm. (with small leaves) are now included within this species. It reaches a peak of flowering in the early summer, but can begin to blossom before the leaves appear in the early spring. It has terminal panicles of fragrant lilac flowers which are shorter but broader than those of *B. davidii*. The individual flowers which make up the inflorescence are tubular, about 1 cm long, with four lilac petal lobes shading to orange at the mouth; the 'eye' is white. The four stamens are attached to the corolla tube inside and the anthers are held about the mid-point, just above the stigma. The deciduous leaves are thickly

continued on page 88

18 Cultivated by Mrs H. Dillon, Ranelagh, Dublin, 14 August 1985. [×0.8]

continued

clothed in soft, rusty-white down, so that they appear grey. They are arranged in opposite pairs, each one with a short (about 1 cm long) stalk and a lanceolate blade up to 15 cm and with toothed margins. The stems, which are tetragonal in cross-section, are also covered with a whitish felt.

This shrub is usually grown against a wall, but it does not really require this of support or protection. It is hardy and can reach as tall as 5 m. *B. crispa* can be pruned in spring before the leaves appear, but this delays the blossom and it is preferable to prune after the blossoms have withered. It is tolerant of lime and can be propagated from seeds or from cuttings. Like *B. davidii*, *B. crispa* attracts nectar-seeking insects, especially butterflies, and thus it makes a fine shrub for gardens in which wild creatures are encouraged. If these two species are planted together, the flowering season can be prolonged from June into October.

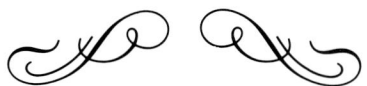

PLATE 19
Lonicera tragophylla Hemsley

PLATE 19
Lonicera tragophylla Hemsley

Caprifoliaceae   golden honeysuckle

Lonicera consists of at least two hundred species of shrubs distributed throughout the northern hemisphere. Some are free-standing, but the genus includes many climbers – the native honeysuckle (*L. periclymenum* L.) is a familiar example.

China has been the source of many excellent garden plants and several species of *Lonicera* introduced from China are now widely cultivated. The small-leaved *L. nitida* Wils., which is so amenable to trimming as a hedge, is one of the Chinese native species; it is rarely seen flowering here because it is trimmed, but it produces small, pallid-cream flowers in June. *L. pileata* Oliv. is also a Chinese species – it is widely used as an evergreen ground-cover shrub – and is one of a group of honeysuckles discovered by Dr Augustine Henry.

Dr Henry's reputation as a botanical collector is widely known; examples of his discoveries include *Lilium henryi* Baker (AIF I: Plate 43), *Rhododendron augustinii* Hemsl. (AIF I: Plate 46) and *Lonicera henryi* Hemsl. He also found this magnificent honeysuckle in the Patung district of Hubei province in central China. *L. tragophylla* is noted by Henry in his pamphlet, *Notes on economic botany of China*, published in 1893 to encourage missionaries and others to help explore the riches of the Chinese flora.

Lonicera tragophylla is a twining vine, scrambling through shrubs; in cultivation it requires the support of a trellis or pergola. The leaves, as in all honeysuckles, are arranged in opposite pairs (the lower ones are separate but those near the flowers are fused into a single, stem-encircling collar) and they are up to 10 cm long and 5 cm broad, glabrous above but downy beneath, especially on the mid-vein, with a glaucous bloom which is most pronounced underneath. The young leaves are tinged with purple, and this tint remains until about flowering time. The flowering heads are borne on short side shoots and each one contains about ten individual blooms. This species has beautiful golden-yellow flowers reaching about 10 cm, the longest among the hardy honeysuckles. Each flower is trumpet-shaped, the floral tube made up from five fused petals which at the mouth form two lips, the upper one with four lobes and the lower with a single lobe. The five stamens project from the mouth of the flower as the long style. The fruits are small, red berries.

This lovely honeysuckle is not fragrant – the great English gardener E. A. Bowles wrote that its failure to produce a perfume was 'rather disgraceful for a Honeysuckle but forgivable in one so daffodilious in hue.'

Lonicera tragophylla is hardy, but it is not at all common in gardens and is rarely stocked by nurserymen. It thrives in a rich loam, preferring a position where its shoots are in the open but where its roots and lower stems are shaded from the hottest sun.

Although discovered by Dr Henry, this honeysuckle was introduced by Ernest Wilson and flowered for the first time in Europe at Messrs Veitch's nursery, Coombe Wood, in 1904.

19 Cultivated by David Shackleton, Clonsilla, County Dublin, 9 July 1984. [×0.6]

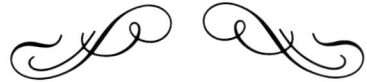

PLATE 20

Oxypetalum coeruleum (D. Don) Decaisne

(syn. *Tweedia coerulea* D. Don; *T. versicolor* W. J. Hooker)

PLATE 20

Oxypetalum coeruleum (D. Don) Decaisne

(syn. *Tweedia coerulea* D. Don; *T. versicolor* W. J. Hooker)

Asclepiadaceae   Tweedia

Oxypetalum coeruleum is a native of Brazil and Uruguay, and was discovered and introduced into European gardens by a Scottish horticulturist and plant collector, John Tweedie. It flowered at Gillan's nursery, Shacklewell Lane, London, during June 1837, and at the Royal Dublin Society's Botanic Gardens, Glasnevin, in July 1837 for the first time outside its native land. David Don named the plant in Robert Sweet's *British Flower Garden*; an illustration was published in November 1837.

Tweedie had sent seeds to several contacts in Britain and Ireland under the name 'Asclepias asedra', but Ninian Niven, curator of the Glasnevin Botanic Gardens, had not seen any plant like it before and reckoned that it was not a species of *Asclepias*. As it was not recorded in journals or floras, and was 'so rare and beautiful', Niven sent a drawing of the plant and some fresh specimens to Dr William Hooker, then Professor of Botany in the University of Glasgow. Hooker recognized it as an unnamed species of the genus *Tweedia* which he and George Arnott had described in 1834 and named 'in compliment to [John Tweedie] an intelligent and indefatigable collector of plants'; Hooker gave it the binomial *T. versicolor*.

Sometimes the best intentions of botanists in commemorating their friends and helpers come to nought because opinions change and rules demand that names be abandoned. Hooker noted that the known species of *Tweedia* were similar to species of *Oxypetalum*, and botanists now agree that *Tweedia* is not a distinct genus. It was merged with *Oxypetalum* by Joseph Decaisne in 1844, and as the generic name *Oxypetalum* and the epithet *coerulea* were published first, they take priority; thus *T. versicolor* has been renamed *Oxypetalum coeruleum*.

John Tweedie is not now immortalized with an accepted genus, but there are a number of South American species named after him and it is still perfectly acceptable to use the name Tweedia as a vernacular name for this beautiful blue-flowered plant.

Oxypetalum coeruleum is a hirsute perennial with thin, trailing branches which become slightly woody as they age. The greyish-green leaves are arranged in opposite pairs; they are lanceolate with a cordate base and acute apex, about 4 cm long and 2 cm broad. The sky-blue flowers are borne towards the tips of the shoots in axillary clusters. Each flower has five strap-shaped corolla lobes fused at the base into a short tube at the mouth of which there is a raised five-lobed corona, slightly darker in colour than the corolla lobes. There are five stamens and a single pistil. After pollination, a large fruit is formed resembling a dumpy broad-bean; the cylindrical pod is tapered towards the base and apex and is packed with seeds, each bearing a feathery pappus.

This plant is not hardy and is usually treated as a perennial for the cold glasshouse; it can be placed out-of-doors during the summer and might survive in some of the milder Irish gardens in a well-sheltered place. It can be raised from seeds and will flower within twelve months. Indoors, it blooms in early spring and through most of the summer.

John Tweedie was a native of Scotland who emigrated to the Argentine in 1824; he died in Buenos Aires on 1 April 1862. He supplied Glasnevin Botanic Gardens with countless packages of seeds between about 1834 and his death. From these many new plants were raised and his most memorable introduction is the pampas grass, *Cortaderia selloana* (Schultes & Schultes) Asch. & Graebn., which flowered at Glasnevin in 1842 and was distributed from there to other European gardens.

On 26 May 1836, after learning that a genus had been named in his honour, the modest Mr Tweedie wrote to Professor William Hooker: 'My thanks is also due to you & Mr Arnold [*sic*] for inrolling my name among the imortle list of eminent Botanists. I regret much that I did not leorn more in my youthfull years to enable me to mearit such, but following after little mor than cabbage planting nor aspiring at more I of course are badly prepared for sientific porsuits.'

20 Cultivated by Mrs W. F. Walsh, Lusk, County Dublin, 25 July 1985 (flowering shoot) and Mrs V. Keegan, Bray, County Wicklow, 12 October 1985 (fruit). [×0.65]

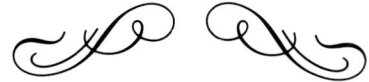

PLATE 21

Dionaea muscipula Ellis

PLATE 21
Dionaea muscipula Ellis

Saxifragaceae   Venus fly-trap, tipitiwitchet

My Good Friend Collinson,

    I ask pardon for not answering y^r Letter so long ago received, but my chagrin for all the seeds I had collected for you and my other Friends by their being cast away near Boloign [Boulogne] discouraged my sending over any more During the war, and my Removal to this place and being taken up in planting, and Building, draining, fencing, &c I have had no time yet of turning my thoughts to Botany.... I sent you over some sensitive Bryar seed but cant tell if you received it. We have a kind of a Catch Fly Sensitive which closes upon any thing that touches it. It grows in the Latitude 34, but none in 35°. I will try to save the seed. My son who carries this will inform you more particularly what relates to this Province and produce here to whom I refer you, and [I] am with truth,

    My good Friend
      Yr Most Humble Servant
        Arthur Dobbs.

That letter, written from Brunswick in North Carolina on 2 April 1759 by Governor Arthur Dobbs to the London botanist Peter Collinson, contained the first intimation of the existence of the remarkable plant called the tipitiwitchet. A few months later, on 24 January 1760, in response we may assume to an enquiry about it from Collinson, Governor Dobbs added this description: 'But the great wonder of the vegetable kingdom is a very curious unknown species of sensitive; it is a dwarf plant; the leaves are like a narrow segment of a sphere, consisting of two parts like the cap of a spring purse, the concave part outwards, each of which falls back with indented edges (like an iron spring fox trap); upon anything touching the leaves, or falling between them, they instantly close like a spring trap and confine any insect or anything that falls between them; it bears a white flower: to this surprising plant I have given the name of Fly Trap Sensitive.'

This whetted the appetite of Collinson and other European naturalists who were ever anxious to acquire new plants, and various attempts were made to send the Fly Trap Sensitive from North Carolina. Arthur Dobbs showed the strange plant to John Bartram, America's leading naturalist, in 1762; William, John's son, was later to describe the plant as 'this sportive vegetable.... Astonishing production! see the incarnate lobes expanding, how gay and ludicrous they appear! ready on the spring to intrap incautious deluded insects, what artifice! there behold one of the leaves just closed upon a struggling fly, another has got a worm, its hold is sure, its prey can never escape – carnivorous vegetable! ... we see here, in this plant, motion and volition.'

After his visit to Dobbs, John Bartram returned to Philadelphia with living specimens of the fly-trap, and he set about trying to send plants to his friend in England. Thomas Fisher was entrusted with this task during the winter of 1762/1763, but he does not appear to have succeeded, although every letter between Bartram and Collinson included some mention of the fly-trap. Living plants or seeds seem to have arrived in England before June 1764, for on 1 June, Peter Collinson wrote to Bartram saying that 'I want to go to Gordon's [nursery at Mile End, London], to see if he has any luck with the Tipitiwitchet...'. Certainly by 1768, the fly-trap was established in English gardens and its successful introduction is usually attributed to William Young, Bartram's competitor.

Tipitiwitchet and fly-trap sensitive were not names that could be used by pedantic scientists, most of whom had recently accepted the system of binomial Latin names proposed by the eminent Swedish botanist Carl von Linné (Linnaeus). Once specimens were available for botanists to study and describe, this 'ludicrous' plant could be given a binomial Latin name. The person who had the privilege of naming it was John Ellis, and he chose to call the curious vegetable *Dionaea muscipula* – Venus's fly-trap. And Linnaeus exclaimed that it was *Miraculum naturae*!

The two men most directly connected with *Dionaea* were both Irish. John Ellis, agent for the Linen Board, was born somewhere in the north of Ireland – his origins are obscure. He lived in London for many years and became one of the most significant amateur naturalists in the

continued on page 100

---

21 Cultivated by Mrs W. F. Walsh, Lusk, County Dublin (plant with bud, 1 May 1984; plant in flower, 15 June 1984) and Dr E. C. Nelson, Celbridge, County Kildare (third plant, 1 October 1984). [×0.75]

continued

late eighteenth century. He had a particular interest in corallines, and wrote instructions for the transport of plants from distant lands. A correspondent of Linnaeus, John Ellis was the person who conveyed the news of *Dionaea* to the Swedish botanist on 23 September 1768: 'Inclosed I send you a print of a very curious sensitive plant. About 3 years ago poor Collinson recd. from John Bartram a dry specimen of this plant. [Dr Daniel] Solander dissected it at my Chambers and from the peculiar appearance of its leaves called it Dione: but Solander being gone [to the South Seas] and his description lockd up with the rest of his papers a few days ago I recd a plant in flower [brought lately from] America from whence the inclosed plate is designd and have attempted to give the Characters of this new Genus ... I think the name Dionaea better than Dione.'

Arthur Dobbs, who gave the first account of the tipitiwitchet, was the son of Richard and Mary Dobbs of Castle Dobbs near Carrickfergus in County Antrim. He was born on 2 April 1689 at Girvan in Scotland, where his mother was prudently sheltering while the armies of King William III and King James II skirmished in Ireland. After his father's death, Arthur Dobbs inherited the family estates in Antrim and he took a special interest in planting orchards and woodlands to improve them. In 1727 he was elected to the Irish Parliament and in 1732, true to the ideas he espoused, Dobbs was among the fourteen gentlemen who formed the society known today as the Royal Dublin Society. But he had grander schemes in mind, and in 1745 purchased land in North Carolina. Six years later, he applied to become governor of North Carolina, was appointed and eventually arrived in America in October 1754. He died in Town Creek, North Carolina, on 28 March 1765.

Dionaea muscipula is a small herb whose remarkable leaves grow in a rosette. Flowering takes place in summer, when a tall stem rises from the leaf-rosette bearing a cluster of about six white flowers, each formed from five green-veined and translucent petals; there are also five green sepals. There are about twenty stamens and a single ovary crowned with a compound stigma.

The leaves can fold in half lengthways, their long marginal teeth — beautifully described by John Ellis as being 'stiff hairs like the Eyebrows' — interlocking perfectly to form a secure prison. On the inner surface of each half of the leaf there are three colourless bristles which act as the triggers springing the trap. When an object — usually a fly — touches one of these hairs twice, a set of reactions takes place which results in the rapid folding of the leaf. The precise method by which the signal is transmitted from the trigger-hair to the cells that, by collapsing, cause the leaf to react, is not understood. The insect is sometimes crushed by the closing leaf, but, if not, it will surely die inside the sealed trap.

Insects are attracted to the leaves by nectar which is secreted from cells around the margin of each leaf. The red pigmentation of the inner surface of the leaf, which intensifies in bright sunlight, also acts as a lure. After an insect is trapped, acids and digestive enzymes are produced by special glands, and these aid in the digestion of the insect's tissues. The nutrients released as the tissues are broken down are absorbed by the plant.

Venus fly-trap is a popular plant because of its remarkable moving leaves and its unsavoury habits. In its native habitats in North Carolina, it grows in damp, sandy soil, so in cultivation it should be grown in a mixture of sharp sand and peat (equal proportions of each) in a tall pot, so that the plants can form a good root system. The pot must stand on a wide, water-filled saucer so that there is a humid atmosphere around the plant. Only rainwater should be used. *D. muscipula* is best grown indoors, either on a sunny windowsill or in a cool greenhouse, but it should be able to survive out-of-doors in mild southern gardens. If carefully tended, this is one of the easiest of the carnivorous plants to grow.

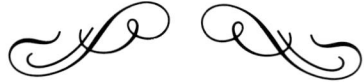

PLATE 22

Olearia 'Henry Travers'

(*Olearia semidentata* Decaisne misapplied)

PLATE 22
Olearia 'Henry Travers'
(*Olearia semidentata* Decaisne misapplied)

Asteraceae   Chatham Island daisy-bush

In October 1908 a case full of living plants arrived in Dublin from Wellington, New Zealand. They had been sent by Henry Travers to the Botanic Gardens at Glasnevin as part of an arrangement between Travers and Frederick Moore, Keeper of the Gardens. All the plants which survived the very long voyage to Ireland were of species that are endemic to New Zealand or the Chatham Islands; included in the consignment were several plants believed to represent *Olearia semidentata*, a beautiful, large-blossomed daisy-bush found only in the Chatham Islands and not in cultivation in Europe at that period. The plants flourished at Glasnevin. A small, pressed specimen of this daisy-bush, now in the herbarium of the Royal Botanic Gardens, Kew, indicates that the shrub bloomed in Dublin during the early summer of 1910.

But that specimen is not exactly like the original (type) specimen of *O. semidentata*, nor are any of the plants grown in gardens throughout Ireland and Britain today. They have longer, broader leaves and pubescent phyllaries, while *O. semidentata* has almost glabrous phyllaries and relatively short, narrow leaves. Thus the plants cultivated as *O. semidentata* probably represent a hybrid between that species and another, closely related, Chatham Island endemic, *O. chathamica* T. Kirk.

It is widely reported that *O. semidentata* was introduced into cultivation in Europe by Captain Arthur Dorrien-Smith in 1910, when he brought young plants to Tresco in the Isles of Scilly, but the fine illustration of his plant, published during April 1914 in *Curtis's Botanical Magazine* (tab. 8550), shows that he also had been growing the hybrid. Indeed, while he certainly gathered and dried specimens of the true *O. semidentata*, he does not appear to have brought plants of it to Tresco. Perhaps he was attracted by the larger flowers of the hybrid, for those of the true *O. semidentata* are not as showy as the flowers of either *O. chathamica* or the hybrids.

Thus the scanty evidence available suggests that the true *O. semidentata* has never been cultivated in Ireland or Britain. The plants grown under that name should be named *Olearia* 'Henry Travers', a name given in recognition of Travers' priority in this horticultural tale.

Olearia 'Henry Travers' forms a broad, rounded shrub up to 3 m tall in its native habitats. In congenial coastal gardens, it grows even taller – the shrubs in Dr David Robinson's garden at Howth are over 4 m in height with robust trunks. The foliage is evergreen and concentrated at the tips of the shoots. The leaves are lanceolate, tapering to a pointed apex and without an obvious stalk; they are up to 14 cm long and not more than 4 cm broad. The upper surface is dark glossy green, but underneath the leaf is coated with a dense mat of silvery-white hairs. The leaf margins are bluntly toothed and slightly inrolled. As this is a member of the daisy family (Asteraceae), the individual flowers are minute and are grouped into a capitulum with pale-lilac ray florets and rich-purple disc florets. The inflorescence is about 7 cm in diameter and held on a long stalk.

Henry Travers, the introducer of this marvellous shrub into Irish gardens, was the son of William Thomas Locke Travers, a native of Limerick who emigrated to New Zealand in 1849, five years after his son was born. William Travers was a barrister, member of parliament and judge of the Supreme Court in Canterbury, New Zealand. Henry studied law and practised as a lawyer in Wellington, but he maintained a strong interest in botany, a hobby which he shared with his father. He made a botanical expedition to the Chatham Islands in 1863, and in later years also explored the provinces of Canterbury and Marlborough. He returned to the Chatham Islands in 1871. After retiring, Henry Travers tried to earn a living by exporting live plants which he collected in the wild. Glasnevin Botanic Gardens received several consignments from him in the early 1900s, but the cost of shipping crates loaded with plants, combined with the high percentage of deaths during the long sea voyage, discouraged him and he gave up sending living plants in 1910.

continued on page 104

22 Cultivated by Dr David Robinson, Howth, County Dublin, 30 July 1985. [×0.7]

continued

Henry Travers and his father are commemorated in many New Zealand species and in one genus *Traversia* (Asteraceae), dedicated by Joseph Hooker to William Travers. *Olearia traversii* F. Mueller and *Geranium traversii* J. D. Hooker are possibly the best known of these eponymous New Zealand endemics.

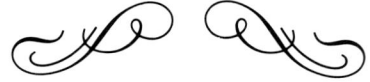

PLATE 23

Crinum moorei J. D. Hooker

PLATE 23
Crinum moorei J. D. Hooker

Amaryllidaceae   Moore's lily, boslelie

Crinum is a large genus of bulbous perennials containing over one hundred species which are widely distributed throughout subtropical and tropical regions. None is native in Europe, although the related genus *Pancratium* is represented by two species which inhabit sandy beaches in southern Europe.

This elegant lily, named after Dr David Moore who was Director of Glasnevin Botanic Gardens, is a native of Natal and the Eastern Cape Province in South Africa. It was introduced into cultivation through Glasnevin in 1863 by Mr Webb, about whom little is known except that he was on the commissariat staff of the British Army and was serving in South Africa at that time. The lily was not named when Mr Webb sent it to Dublin.

Dr Moore had some bulbs of this *Crinum* planted in the border in front of the magnificent Curvilinear Range at Glasnevin. These flowered for the first time in 1869 and five years later, Dr Joseph Hooker, who was David Moore's counterpart in the Royal Botanic Gardens, Kew, named and described the species, basing his protologue on material supplied from Glasnevin. According to Hooker's original account and to a later report by Frederick Moore, who succeeded his father as curator in Glasnevin, the bulbs were not afforded any protection during the winter months. They were, however, planted deeply; Frederick Moore recommended 3 ft (about 1 m) as the ideal depth.

Illustrations of Dr Moore's lily were published in *Curtis's Botanical Magazine* and *The Garden* in 1874 and 1881 respectively, and a photograph taken about 1914 of the original group of *C. moorei* is extant. From these it has been possible to confirm that the clump of *C. moorei* which today grows in front of the Curvilinear Range is the original one, and the material used in preparing the painting for *An Irish Florilegium* came from this group.

Crinum moorei still receives no winter protection at Glasnevin, although it must be stressed that heat seeping from the glasshouse undoubtedly assists in reducing the damaging effects of prolonged frost. No special treatment is given to the lily, except benign neglect; no mulch or compost is ever applied and the bulbs are never disturbed. As Glasnevin is not a particularly mild garden, it may be concluded that *C. moorei* is hardy, and if planted deeply in well-drained soil, it will thrive and flower every year.

The bulb of this *Crinum* is about 15 cm in diameter with a prolonged neck which in cultivated plants may be as much as 50 cm long, but in wild plants only about 12 cm. The leaves are bright pale green with prominent parallel veins; in Irish conditions they are up to 10 cm broad and in a good season can be almost 1 m long. The leaf margins are undulate. From each bulb rises a single flowering stalk; in Glasnevin these can be 2 m tall in an ideal season. The stalk is slightly flattened in cross-section and at its apex bears a cluster of flowers which are at first enclosed in spathe-valves, the whole resembling a stout spear. These valves, pale green tinged with red, split as the flower-buds swell and then remain hanging from the tip of the stalk. Each flower – there can be up to ten flowers on each flowering spike – is held on a short pedicel (about 2 cm long) and is composed of an ovary and a slender tube (about 10 cm long) which eventually swells into a pointed, ovoid bud. The bud is a beautiful pink, but as it opens this colour slowly fades until the six large petals are almost white. The flowers open in slow succession, so that for four weeks there is always a fresh white trumpet atop each bulb. The individual flowers have six stamens; the longest of the curving filaments are about 7 cm and all are tinged with pink.

Crinum moorei is not commonly available in commerce, but it is grown in numerous gardens in Ireland, Britain and Europe. However, the most abundantly cultivated *Crinum* is a hybrid between *C. moorei* and *C. bulbispermum* (Burm.) Milne-Redhead & Schweickerdt (formerly *C. capense* auct. non Herbert), named *C.* × *powellii* Baker after C. Baden Powell of Southborough, Tonbridge, Kent, who deliberately cross-pollinated the parents in 1875. *C.* × *powellii* is hardier than Dr Moore's species, and exists in several colour forms ranging from pure white to deep pink.

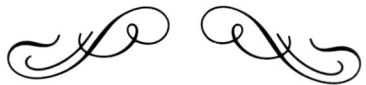

PLATE 24

Littonia modesta W. J. Hooker

PLATE 24
Littonia modesta W. J. Hooker

Liliaceae climbing bell, geelklokkie

It was, and is, a common practice among plant taxonomists to commemorate their fellow botanists by devising new names for genera and species which incorporate the surname (or more rarely the first name) of the dedicatees. Thus Sir William Hooker gave to a genus of climbing lilies from Arabia and Africa the name *Littonia* as 'a tribute to the late Dr Samuel Litton, for twenty-one years Professor of Botany in the Royal Dublin Society, a deeply learned and amiable man, and a popular lecturer'.

Samuel Litton (1781–1847) was a native of London, but spent his childhood in Lancashire. At the age of fourteen he came to Dublin as a scholar in Trinity College. His undergraduate career was distinguished and he graduated in 1800. After a period studying medicine at the University of Edinburgh, he came back to Dublin, and in 1815 was elected Librarian to the Royal Dublin Society. Following the death of the Society's first Professor of Botany, Dr Walter Wade, in 1825, Dr Litton was elected to that position and he thus served as the principal scientist in the Royal Dublin Society's Botanic Gardens at Glasnevin. Despite his accomplishments as an undergraduate in the University, Samuel Litton did not become a distinguished botanist – he published no original research – but he was widely respected as a competent lecturer. He died in 1847 and was succeeded as Professor of Botany by Dr William Henry Harvey.

Harvey spent several years as Colonial Treasurer in Cape Town and during his time at the Cape of Good Hope he carried out substantial botanical studies. He also stimulated other residents to collect plants and thereby formed a small group of amateur collectors in Natal and Cape Province. One of Dr Harvey's contacts, John Sanderson, was responsible for the discovery of *Littonia* and its introduction into cultivation in Europe. Mr Sanderson was himself commemorated in another genus of the Liliaceae – *Sandersonia* W. J. Hooker.

Littonia comprises about seven species native in tropical Africa and Arabia; the single species native in southern Africa was named *L. modesta* because Hooker thought that 'the modest appearance of this plant, in contrast with its very near ally the *Gloriosa superba* Linn., may further serve to indicate [Dr Litton's] unassuming and retiring disposition, which, as has been recorded by the Council of the Royal Dublin Society, "prevented him taking the rank in general society to which his acquirements entitled him".'

Littonia modesta climbs by means of tendrils which are simply prolonged leaf apices that curl around the twigs and stems of neighbouring plants – in cultivation the stems may be supported by canes. The leaves are sessile, ovate, bright green and devoid of hairs; they are arranged in whorls, usually of three. The stems which are produced from a strangely shaped brown tuber – it resembles a small truffle – are terete and rise to about 1 m in height in cultivation. The elegant orange flowers are composed of six identical sepals which are 2 cm long and about 1 cm broad with an acute apex. The individual flowers are pendulous and are formed at the nodes on the upper part of the stem. There are six stamens and a single trilobed style. The ovary is composed of three fused carpels.

This is not an easy plant to keep in cultivation. The plant depicted in our plate was raised from tubers supplied by the National Botanic Garden, Kirstenbosch (South Africa). Flowers were produced about three months after the tubers had been planted. The lily was grown in a pot in a sandy compost and in a heated glasshouse. It is unlikely that *L. modesta* would survive out-of-doors in Ireland except in the mildest gardens in County Kerry, but as far as is known this has never been attempted.

Littonia modesta is widely distributed in South Africa but is absent from Cape Province. Max Leichtlin, an enthusiastic horticulturist who lived in Baden-Baden, obtained some tubers of *L. modesta* from Wilhelm Keit, curator of the Natal Botanic Garden, Durban, in the early 1880s; these apparently produced flowers which Leichtlin thought were larger than usual and he named the variant after Keit – *L. modesta* var. *keitii* Leichtlin. Julius Wilhelm Keit was propagator in Glasnevin Botanic Gardens before emigrating to Natal in 1874.

24 Cultivated in National Botanic Gardens, Glasnevin, Dublin (ex National Botanic Garden, Kirstenbosch, Cape Province, South Africa), 21 November 1984. [×0.6]

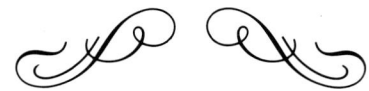

PLATE 25

Mackaya bella Harvey

PLATE 25
Mackaya bella Harvey

Acanthaceae

John Sanderson (see Plate 24) discovered this shrub at Kruis Fontein in the valley of the River Tongat, Natal. He collected specimens, pressed and dried them, and sent them to Professor William Harvey at Trinity College, Dublin. Harvey recognized that the specimens represented a new genus and he decided to describe it; this was done in 1859 in the *Proceedings of the Dublin University Zoological and Botanical Association*. Dr Harvey chose to name it after his friend and colleague, Dr James Townsend Mackay, who served as curator of the University's Botanical Garden at Ballsbridge from its formation in 1806 until his death in 1862.

This was not the first time that Mackay had been honoured in this manner. In 1821 Samuel Gray named a genus of the brown seaweeds (Phaeophyceae) *Mackaia*, but the name was superfluous and was soon abandoned. George Arnott used *Mackaya* in 1838 for a tropical liane which is now placed in the genus *Erythropalum* (Erythropalaceae). There were other, more mundane, honours; the University of Dublin recognized J. T. Mackay's contribution to the study of botany in Ireland and his services as curator of the College Botanic Garden by awarding him the honorary degree of LL.B. in 1850.

Mackaya bella is easily cultivated in a greenhouse which is heated in late winter; tropical conditions are not required, although *Mackaya* will thrive in high temperatures; there is a magnificent shrub, over 3 m tall, in the Tropical Ravine in the Royal Botanic Gardens Park, Belfast. It flowers every spring, often beginning to bloom in February and continuing for several months. The plant was introduced into Europe through the Royal Botanic Gardens, Kew, by its discoverer John Sanderson and by Mark McKen, who was curator of Natal Botanic Garden, Durban. It first flowered in the Palm House at Kew in 1869.

This shrub is easy to propagate — semi-hardwood cuttings, dipped in rooting hormone, will root within a few weeks. Once rooted, they should be potted into a rich loam and kept watered. If well nourished and given heat in the winter — a minimum temperature of 12°C is recommended — these young plants should flower in their first year. *M. bella* has been planted out-of-doors at Rossdohan in County Kerry, but it is unlikely that the species could survive elsewhere in Ireland throughout the winter without protection.

Mackaya bella is a scrambling shrub in its native habitat. The shoots are dark green when young, and light grey when mature. The leaves are elliptical with a prolonged apex and undulating margins; they are glossy dark green above and paler beneath. The largest leaves are about 15 cm long and about 6 cm broad. The flowers are grouped in a racemose inflorescence produced at the ends of the previous year's shoots; the individual blossoms, which resemble the flowers of the European foxglove (*Digitalis purpurea* L.) in form, are pale lavender with very fine darker markings. Each flower has a small, five-lobed calyx and five petals fused into a bell-shaped corolla about 5 cm long; the upper two lobes of the corolla are the smaller ones, and the central, lower lobe is the largest. The two lateral lobes are held almost horizontally and spread about 4 cm; they are slightly recurved at maturity. There are two fertile stamens bearing anthers — these are fused to the corolla tube and each has a pilose anther at the tip of the filament. There are also two infertile staminodes which have no anthers. The ovary has two locules and is surmounted by a thin style with a minute, two-lobed stigma.

Mackaya is a monotypic genus. The single species has sometimes been assigned to *Asystasia* Blume, but modern opinion holds that this South African plant does represent a distinct, endemic genus. Because of Gray's and Arnott's earlier publication of the names *Mackaia* and *Mackaya*, Harvey's generic name has been conserved under the International Code of Botanical Nomenclature.

James Townsend Mackay is also commemorated in the native Irish heather *Erica mackaiana* Bab. (AIF I: Plate 15).

Several other botanists associated with Trinity College, Dublin, were granted immortality among the names of plants. Robert Scott, Professor of Botany from 1785 until 1808, had the

continued on page 116

25 Cultivated in Royal Botanic Gardens Park, Belfast, County Antrim, 14 March 1986. [×0.6]

continued

genus *Scottia* (now placed in *Bossiaea* Vent. (Papilionaceae)) named after him by Robert Brown. *Burbidgea*, a member of the ginger family (Zingiberaceae), is a memorial to Frederick William Burbidge, who was one of Mackay's successors (1879–1905) as curator of the College Gardens. Frederick Moore, Burbidge's predecessor, is commemorated in a genus of orchids, *Neomoorea* Rolfe, and the name *Moorea* was twice attempted, once for David Moore and later for Frederick. Professor Harvey has the parasitic genus *Harveya* (Scrophulariaceae) named for him, and his immediate predecessor as Professor of Botany, William Allman, was granted immortality by Robert Brown in the genus *Allmania* (Amaranthaceae). *Romneya coulteri* Harvey (AIF I: Plate 40) is a memorial to two Trinity men, Dr Thomas Romney Robinson, astronomer, and Dr Thomas Coulter, botanist and curator of the College herbarium; the genus *Coulteria* Kunth (Caesalpinaceae) also commemorated Dr Coulter. To mark the bicentenary of the University, Ferdinand von Mueller named *Velleia salmoniana* F. Muell. (Goodeniaceae), a small herb from Western Australia, after the College's Provost, mathematician and divine, Dr George Salmon (1819–1904).

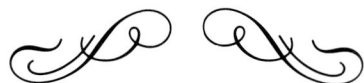

PLATE 26

Abutilon vitifolium (Cavanilles) Presl

(syn. *Corynabutilon vitifolium* (Cavanilles) Kearns)

PLATE 26
Abutilon vitifolium (Cavanilles) Presl
(syn. *Corynabutilon vitifolium* (Cavanilles) Kearns)

Malvaceae

Some botanists take a broad view of the genus *Abutilon* and include about one hundred and fifty species within it. However, there are some taxonomists who conclude that *Abutilon* should be divided into several smaller genera, and they place this species within *Corynabutilon*. *Corynabutilon* differs from *Abutilon* in possessing flattened and club-shaped style branches with the stigmatic surfaces along each edge. While the differences are real, they seem insufficient to warrant the segregation of the species so distinguished, and most authorities retain this species within *Abutilon*.

Captain Edward Cottingham, who lived at Bellfield, on Goosegreen Avenue in Drumcondra, one of Dublin's northern suburbs, was the first person to grow *A. vitifolium* in Europe. It is recorded that he obtained the seeds of this plant in 1836 from Chile, where it is native, but the precise locality and the name of the collector are not known. Four years later, James Townsend Mackay, curator of the College Botanic Garden, Ballsbridge, sent a specimen to Sydenham Edwards, publisher of the journal *Botanical Register*, and he published a coloured illustration of it. Mackay noted that the plant from which the flowers and leaves had been picked had grown out-of-doors in a south-facing border for three years without damage. Captain Cottingham gave one plant to the Royal Horticultural Society of London for its garden at Chiswick in 1839.

Abutilon vitifolium is not completely hardy in Ireland, probably because it grows quickly and does not form tough, woody stems. It can reach over 5 m in height in sheltered, congenial gardens, but sooner or later it will be either damaged by frost or toppled by strong winds. Even when tree-like in dimensions, it is little more than a very large herbaceous perennial with soft shoots. The young shoots, leaf- and flower-stalks are all cloaked in a fawn felt. The leaves are evergreen in mild areas, but deciduous elsewhere. They are, as the specific epithet indicates, vine-like with five lobes, the central one the largest; they are covered with fine, white hairs and thus are grey-green in colour. The shrub begins to blossom in May and may continue to bloom for several months; its flowers vary in colour from mauve-blue to almost pure white, but Captain Cottingham's original plant had white flowers 'with a slight tinge of blush'. Such colour forms exist today, and like the one in our painting, they are pale mauve with feathery, bright-mauve styles and golden-orange anthers. The flowers are grouped in a loose panicle and are borne towards the tips of the branches. The fruit is disc-like, composed of about ten fused carpels, each carpel containing several black seeds.

This species can be raised easily from seeds, but the colours of the flowers may vary. If a particular colour form is wanted, cuttings should be taken in late summer but rooting may be erratic. *A. vitifolium* is tolerant of lime, and will grow in any soil except perhaps damp peat. It will be damaged by severe frosts and is particularly susceptible, in Ireland, to prolonged cold east winds.

Captain Cottingham exhibited his *A. vitifolium* before the council of the Royal Horticultural Society of Ireland in 1840, and the council unanimously approved the award of the Society's Gold Medal to him for his introduction. He distributed the plant to other gardens, and it was therefore being widely cultivated by 1844 when William Lobb, a collector working for Messrs Veitch, sent more seeds from Chile.

26 Cultivated by Dr E. C. Nelson, Celbridge, County Kildare, 27 July 1985, and Professor and Mrs B. Boydell, Baily, Howth, 30 July 1985. [×0.6]

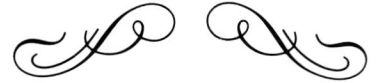

PLATE 27
Rosa bracteata Wendl

PLATE 27
Rosa bracteata Wendl

Rosaceae									Lord Macartney's rose

In the second edition of William Aiton's *Hortus Kewensis* published in 1810, this rose is called Staunton's rose after Sir George Staunton, who was a native of Cargin in County Galway. Sir George, a trained physician, collected it while he was attached to the famous Embassy from King George III to the Emperor Qianlong which arrived at Beijing in August 1793; he was Secretary to the Embassy and Minister Plenipotentiary in the absence of the Ambassador.

The Ambassador Extraordinary and Minister Plenipotentiary was the distinguished and experienced diplomat Lord Macartney of Lisanoure in County Antrim, who was unkindly described by one person as a member of the 'bog-gentry of northern Ireland'. Lord Macartney's name is now attached to this rose and Sir George Staunton is all but forgotten.

In diplomatic terms, the visit to the Celestial Empire was not a success – Lord Macartney did not achieve his objectives and he was curtly but politely dismissed by the Emperor.

However, such embassies were never just diplomatic missions and this one was no exception. There were two gardeners attached to it and Sir Joseph Banks, who directed the King's garden at Kew, issued instructions about plant collecting; he informed Staunton about the rarer plants that might be encountered in China, then little known to western botanists.

David Stronach was the gardener employed by Lord Macartney and John Haxton was personally engaged by Sir George Staunton. They succeeded, during limited excursions into the Chinese countryside, in collecting several hundred dried specimens of plants and some seeds. Among their discoveries were *Rubus reflexus* Ker and *Ilex cornuta* Lindl. The seeds were presented to the Royal Gardens at Kew, where the King's Gardener, William Aiton, worked. Among the plants raised from the Chinese seeds were *Astragalus chinensis* L. f.; *Polygonum chinense* L.; the plume poppy, *Macleaya cordata* (Willd.) R. Br.; and *Rosa bracteata*. Aylmer Bourke Lambert also succeeded in raising plants from seeds brought to England by the Embassy; *Hedysarum latifolium* Roxb. was grown at Boyton House by Lambert.

This rose is a scrambling shrub in its natural habitat; in gardens it is most usually grown as a wall-plant, when it must be trained and wired as it is not capable of climbing. It is evergreen in mild situations and seasons, but in frosty winters the leaves will be killed and fall off. The main shoots are thin, clothed with woolly, white hairs and armed with vicious hooked thorns. The leaves are bright glossy green, with about nine leaflets (four opposite pairs and a larger terminal leaflet). The largest leaflet is about 3 cm long and 2 cm broad. The flowers appear late in the summer and continue into early autumn; they are about 7 cm in diameter and delightfully fragrant, with a perfume reminiscent of lemons. The individual blossoms are white, with five heart-shaped petals, overlapping and forming a bowl-like flower. In the centre is a cluster of golden stamens and the compact column of styles and stigmas. The fruits are crowned by the persistent calyx, and if they ripen are red.

Rosa bracteata is not fully hardy, although it will survive against a south-facing, sheltered wall. Nor is it common in gardens, even though it flowers late in the season after most of the other *Rosa* species have blown. It thrives in a rich loam and is tolerant of lime. Propagation is by cuttings or layering; seeds can be sown, but the rose rarely forms ripe fruits in Ireland due to frost damage in early winter.

Sir George Staunton is commemorated in the genus *Stauntonia*, a climber belonging to the family Lardizabalaceae and related to *Akebia quinata* (Houtt.) Decne. A privet, *Ligustrum sinensis* Lour. var. *stauntonii* (DC.) Rehd., and the bamboo, *Phyllostachys stauntonii* Munro, which are native in China, also bear his name.

Lord Macartney's rose was named *R. macartnea* by Dumont de Coursent in 1805, but the binomial *R. bracteata* published in 1798 has precedence.

27 Cultivated by Dr E. C. Nelson, Celbridge, County Kildare, 6 September 1984. [×0.6]

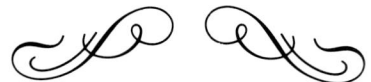

PLATE 28

Rubus lasiostylus Focke

PLATE 28
Rubus lasiostylus Focke

Rosaceae

The genus *Rubus* includes the brambles or blackberries (*R. fruticosus* L. sens. lat.) which are such familiar weedy plants in Ireland. But not all species of *Rubus* have a scrambling habit; there are many species with stouter stems which can form erect shrubs – the raspberry (*R. idaeus* L.) is one example – and some of these brambles make attractive garden plants, especially those with white stems. *R. lasiostylus*, which is akin to the garden raspberry, produces tall, erect canes with a pinkish-white bloom, but it is not well known in gardens.

This beautiful shrub is native in central China and was first collected by Dr Augustine Henry about Patung in the province of Hubei; he sent herbarium specimens to the Royal Botanic Gardens, Kew, and, using that material, the species was described by Wilhelm Focke and illustrated in *Icones Plantarum* in 1891. Henry also sent seeds, which were received at Kew in 1889 and successfully germinated. The first flowers were produced in June 1894. Thus in 1895, another illustration of Dr Henry's raspberry was published, this time based on the living plants that had been raised from Dr Henry's seeds. This is indeed one of the Chinese plants which Henry discovered and introduced.

Rubus lasiostylus grows to about 1.5 m tall; the bristle-covered shoots (canes) are best treated as biennial and should be removed after their second season. The young shoots are beautifully coloured – white tinted with crimson bark, and pink bristles. The shoots have bristles only, but a few hooked thorns occur on the leaf-stalks and on the lateral, flowering branchlets. The leaves are composed of three (rarely five) leaflets. The central, terminal leaflet is the largest and may be broader than long; it is obovate, about 7 cm broad. The lateral leaflets are obovate too, but narrower, to 5 cm long and about 3 cm across. The margins of the leaflets are irregularly and finely toothed. The flowers are grouped in a loose panicle at the tips of side-shoots. Each flower has a persistent green calyx, composed of five lanceolate sepals which are fused at the base, each being about 1 cm long and 0.2 cm broad. The five large petals alternate with the sepals; they are obovate, broader than long, and rich magenta-purple in colour. Like the garden raspberry, *R. lasiostylus* has a cluster of carpels in the centre of each flower, which when ripe form a juicy, salmon-pink raspberry that is edible.

It is a mystery why this species is not much more common in gardens. It has attractive shoots which can equal other white-caned *Rubus* species (for example, *R. cockburniana* Hemsley or *R.* × *vedrariensis* Hort.) as subjects for a winter garden. It is tolerant of lime and is completely hardy. As well as the white canes, it has relatively large, richly coloured flowers, pretty fruits, and pleasing foliage.

Propagation is by division, especially of the suckering shoots – but *R. lasiostylus* is not invasive – and from seeds. It flowers in summer on the previous year's shoots, and canes that have bloomed should be removed in the following spring to ensure that vigorous new shoots develop for the succeeding year.

28 Cultivated in National Botanic Gardens, Glasnevin, Dublin, 3 July 1985. [×0.65]

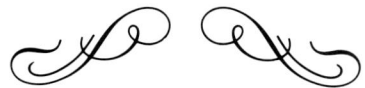

PLATE 29

Helleborus lividus Aiton

PLATE 29
Helleborus lividus Aiton

Ranunculaceae

Helleborus is a genus of about twenty species found in Europe and western Asia; there is also one species in western China. None is native in Ireland, but most of the exotic species are grown in gardens and there are innumerable hybrid cultivars. The familiar white-flowered Christmas rose, *H. niger* L., has been cultivated for many centuries, and was well known to the herb-gatherers of ancient Greece.

Helleborus lividus was grown in the Royal Gardens at Kew, near London, during the 1780s, when it was described and illustrated by William Aiton in one of the early issues of William Curtis's *Botanical Magazine*. Aiton noted that it had been cultivated as early as the beginning of the eighteenth century in the Physic Garden at Chelsea. It seems to have died out in British gardens and by the end of the nineteenth century it was no longer known in cultivation.

It is uncertain if this hellebore had been sent to Ireland at any time before 1900, but it is recorded that Miss Fanny Geoghegan brought some plants of *H. lividus* to Dublin in that year. She had been staying in Majorca, where *H. lividus* is endemic, and had obtained material from its native habitat. In a letter to Frederick Burbidge, curator of the College Botanic Garden at Ballsbridge, she wrote: 'I am sorry to say that I can't really tell you all you want to know about the hellebore – for one thing being an ignoramus on subjects botanical I just sent the plant home as I thought it curious and I wanted to send them something that grew in [Majorca]. To the best of my belief, I saw it growing about the neighbourhood of Pollensa, a village on the north side of the island where among the delightful inhabitants we spent 3 very happy weeks – & as we were constantly accompanied by one or another in our walks, I expect I saw it & said I wanted to get some, for looking today through my diary to see if I had noted anything about it I find "Don Guillemus (he was the schoolmaster) sent me plants of the purple hellebore".'

Burbidge painted Miss Geoghegan's plant on 18 January 1901 – the original watercolour survives in the College Botanic Garden – and in February 1902 and 1903 it bloomed under Burbidge's care in the Botanic Garden. He sent material to the Royal Botanic Gardens, Kew; the specimen was drawn and *H. lividus* was figured for a second time in the *Botanical Magazine*.

It has never been a common plant in gardens; several keen gardeners about Dublin cultivate it today both in cool glasshouses and out-of-doors. It has been grown at Malahide Castle, County Dublin, since about 1971. Lord Talbot de Malahide raised seedlings from seeds collected by Mrs L. F. Ferguson on 30 April 1971 when she and her husband, Dr Keith Ferguson, visited the cliffs near Betlem, Territoria Municipali de Arta, Majorca. On the peninsula north of Betlem, *H. lividus* grows on the northwest-facing cliffs.

Helleborus lividus is a perennial herb up to 0.5 m tall with evergreen, leathery leaves beautifully veined with silver and coloured bronzy-red underneath. The leaves are usually trifoliate, each leaflet being about 15 cm long and about 6 cm broad. The leaf margin is either smooth or sparsely toothed. Flowers are produced from January to March in cultivation and they vary in colour; when fully open, the insides of the flowers are usually greyish-purple tinged with green. In *Helleborus* the conspicuous 'petals' are actually sepals – there are five in each flower – and the true petals, which are green, minute and vase-like, act as nectaries and are situated between the sepals and the stamens. There are numerous stamens with yellow anthers in the centre of each flower surrounding the carpels. In fruit, the outer sepals persist, darkening in colour and forming a collar around the carpels with their long, persistent styles.

This hellebore is apparently hardy in gardens near Dublin, but it can be killed by severe frosts. It is easily cultivated in an alpine house or a frame, and thrives in deep, sandy loam. As in other hellebores, propagation by seed is easy, but care must be taken to prevent hybridization – *H. lividus* readily crosses with *H. corsicus* Willd. (the hybrid is called *H.* × *sternii* Turrill), a taller, coarser species without the elegant marbled leaves. *H. lividus* is related to *H. argutifolius* Vivani, but may be distinguished by white-

continued on page 132

29 Cultivated at Malahide Castle (Talbot Botanic Garden), County Dublin, 25 March 1986 (grown in cool glasshouse). [×0.65]

continued

veined leaves with red backs, by the sparse (or absent) toothing on the leaves, and by its smaller stature. *H. argutifolius* is native in Corsica and Sardinia, and does not occur in the Balearic Island to which the other species is restricted.

Fanny Geoghegan lived at Donabate, County Dublin, for many years where, despite her protestations of botanical ignorance, she grew many rare plants. Among her other achievements was the introduction of the diminutive *Paeonia cambessedesii* Willd. into cultivation, also from Majorca in 1896.

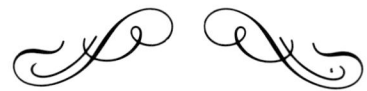

PLATE 30

Anemone coronaria Linnaeus

'Saint Brigid'

PLATE 30
Anemone coronaria Linnaeus
'Saint Brigid'

Ranunculaceae   Saint Brigid anemone

Anemone coronaria, sometimes called the poppy anemone, is a native plant in the eastern Mediterranean region, including Greece and western Asia, and was brought into cultivation in Europe about 1600. In the wild, the plants have red flowers, each bloom being composed of five to eight petaloid perianth segments. In the centre of the flower numerous very dark stamens surround the cluster of carpels. The fruiting head looks like a grey raspberry, and is composed of hundreds of small, ripe carpels, each of which contains a single seed. The individual flowers are solitary, held erect on a single stem which has a ruff of leaf-like bracts below the bloom. The basal leaves emerge from the rootstock about the same time as the flowers; these leaves are deep green, deeply dissected like parsley leaves and have long stalks.

This species is easy to cultivate. It may be raised from seeds, sown in drills or seed pans in summer or winter. Seedlings can be transplanted when large enough to handle, but it is better to sow thinly where the plants are to be grown, so that transplanting is unnecessary. Nowadays the poppy anemone is most usually grown from 'corms' (in strict botanical terms, these are small, tuberous rhizomes). If planted in autumn, flowers will develop the following spring.

The poppy anemone became one of the most popular of the so-called 'florist's flowers' during the eighteenth century, and retained its popularity through the 1800s. As it was frequently raised from seed, colour forms and unusual variants were commonplace, and some of these were selected for further development. One of the most conspicuous variants was the double-flowered one, in which the relatively small number of broad perianth segments was replaced by narrow and more numerous segments, giving each bloom a fuller, somewhat shaggy, appearance. Eventually, two separate strains of the poppy anemone were developed and named – the single-flowered one was called 'De Caen', and the double one 'Saint Brigid'.

Saint Brigid is the patron saint of County Kildare, and her name was adopted as a *nom-de-plume* by Mrs Alice Louisa Lawrenson, a 'lady-amateur gardener and writer', who lived for several years in Kildare before moving to Howth, County Dublin. Mrs Lawrenson's name (*alias* Saint Brigid) is associated with a number of plants which were highly prized at the beginning of this century, especially an excellent white Christmas rose with robust, tall, green stems; *Helleborus niger* L. 'Saint Brigid' was not a plant of her own raising, but came from an old garden in Kildare about the middle of the last century and its true origin was never known. Alice Lawrenson did produce her own new cultivars, including a white tulip and several *Narcissus* (daffodil) seedlings with red coronas, of which 'Lucifer' at least still survives. And she was the person who developed the double-flowered strain of *A. coronaria* that is now called 'Saint Brigid'.

At Howth, Mrs Lawrenson grew *A. coronaria* from seed; she sowed it in spring and was able to gather flowers in September. She raised her double-flowered strain during the 1870s and early 1880s by gathering seeds only from the best plants and using this seed for the next crop of plants; this same technique is still used by plant breeders world-wide. Gradually she obtained plants with bigger, brighter and fuller flowers. In October 1882, Alice Lawrenson sent a bunch of her poppy anemones to William Robinson, editor of *The Garden*, who commented that they were very beautiful. Robinson received another bouquet in April 1884. In May 1885, Mrs Lawrenson gave seeds of her poppy anemone to the Royal (now National) Botanic Gardens at Glasnevin.

By the 1890s, *A. coronaria* 'Saint Brigid' was widely available and popular. On 10 April 1895, Earl Cowper of Hertford received an Award of Merit for the Saint Brigid anemone when he showed it at the Royal Horticultural Society in London. About this time too, William Baylor Hartland of Cork was advertising his own strain of the double-flowered anemone, raised from seeds obtained from Mrs Lawrenson. Other nurserymen also sought to develop their own version of the double-flowered strain, and

continued on page 136

30 Cultivated by George McHugh, Geashill, County Offaly, 17 May 1984. [×0.6]

continued

were able to do this simply by sowing seed from selected plants.

One such nurseryman was William Reamsbottom of Alderborough House, Geashill, County Offaly. Family tradition has it that he found good anemones in the garden at The Doon, Athlone, which was his wife's home, and that he worked on these until he had perfected the Alderborough strain of double-flowered anemones. Such traditions are difficult to prove or contradict, but it is just as probable that Reamsbottom, like Hartland, obtained seeds from Mrs Lawrenson. In 1892, Reamsbottom introduced the Alderborough race, and, according to one writer, he succeeded in increasing both the range of colours from five or seven shades to about thirty, and the percentage of double flowers. A display of the Alderborough anemones at the Royal Horticultural Society of London in May 1902 was awarded a silver-gilt medal, and the cultivar was granted a second Award of Merit. In 1903, William Reamsbottom gained a gold medal for his Saint Brigid anemones at Shrewsbury Show.

Direct descendants of the Alderborough race of *A. coronaria* 'Saint Brigid' are still cultivated at Geashill by smallholders, including George McHugh. There are many different shades, ranging from white through pink to red and a variety of mauves to blue. The plants are raised from seed gathered each year.

Years ago, the flowers were cut for the Dublin market, but nowadays the Geashill anemones are grown for no particular purpose – cheaper, imported flowers have made the crop uneconomic. But the Geashill plants, growing in one of the coldest areas of Ireland, are hardy and vigorous and they could provide breeding stock for the continued development of this still popular garden flower.

PLATE 31

Azara microphylla J. D. Hooker

'Variegata'

PLATE 31
Azara microphylla J. D. Hooker
'Variegata'

Flacourtiaceae

This small South American genus, comprising about ten species, is named after a Spanish scientist and diplomat, José Nicolás Azara (1731–1804). Five different species are cultivated in Ireland, but they are not reliably hardy and grow best in the mild, sheltered gardens of the south and west. They form handsome, evergreen shrubs and small trees and have fragrant flowers which superficially resemble those of *Acacia* (Mimosaceae).

Azara microphylla is perhaps the hardiest species in cultivation. It has small, alternately arranged, oval leaves, the margins of which are ornamented with small teeth. In shape and size, the leaves resemble those of the common hedge-plant *Lonicera nitida* Wils., but the arrangement of the leaves in that shrub is opposite. The main branches are more or less erect, but the leafy shoots are thin and thus they tend to become pendulous, giving the whole shrub a light, feathery appearance. In this species, the flowers are minute and concealed behind the leaves; they hang from the shoots on very short, stout stalks. Each individual flower, not more than 0.3 cm across, is composed of four small stamens with a single, central style and ovary. The petals and sepals are greatly reduced and can only be seen using a hand-lens. While the flowers are almost invisible, they do have a marvellous perfume resembling vanilla.

Several species of *Azara* have yielded variegated sports in cultivation, and this cultivar of *A. microphylla* arose as a branch sport on a shrub growing in Belgrove, William Gumbleton's garden near Cobh, County Cork. It was first mentioned in *The Gardeners' Chronicle* on 19 December 1908, when Samuel Arnott recorded that '*Azara microphylla belgroviana* is a beautifully variegated form of this favourite shrub and the specimen of the type itself at Belgrove is exceedingly large and well developed.'

The original plant of *A. microphylla* 'Variegata' remained in Belgrove until November 1911, when it was sold by William Baylor Hartland of Ard Cairn Nurseries, Ballintemple, County Cork, who was charged with the disposal of 'the unique collection of RARE FLOWERING SHRUBS... collected for the past 40 years by the Late W. E. Gumbleton, Esq.' According to an article published in *New Flora and Silva* in 1929, the original was bought by Richard Beamish, who transferred it to his excellent garden at Ashbourne House, a few kilometres from Belgrove. It is not known when the variegated cultivar was first propagated, but Gumbleton apparently gave cuttings to his friends, for in 1921 Lady Moore noted a 'big, spreading plant... a child of the late Mr. W. E. Gumbleton's original plant' growing at Mount Usher in County Wicklow.

Azara microphylla 'Variegata' has a broad but uneven creamy margin to the leaves; it does not differ in any other way from the normal, green-leaved variant, except that it is slower growing and is perhaps a little more susceptible to damage by frost and cold, east winds. Because of the occasional likelihood of damage during the winter, this cultivar is usually grown against a wall – it is, indeed, a most effective plant when seen against a grey-stone or red-brick wall – but at Mount Usher and in several other mild, sheltered gardens, it thrives in the open and forms a delightful ferny shrub. It will tolerate partial shade and is not intolerant of lime.

The cultivar name 'Belgroviana' used by Arnott was never taken up by horticulturists and the variegated plant has generally been called *A. microphylla* 'Variegata' for over sixty years. To revert to the original name would cause unnecessary confusion in gardens and the horticultural trade, and thus the epithet 'Variegata' should be retained.

31 Cultivated by Mrs A. Bisgood, Enniskerry, County Wicklow: shoot, 6 October 1984; flowering shoot, 6 April 1986. [×0.7]

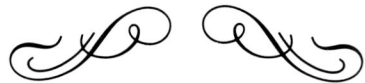

PLATE 32
Rhododendron 'Mulroy Vanguard'

PLATE 32
Rhododendron 'Mulroy Vanguard'

Ericaceae

Although many of Ireland's gardens are renowned for the fine plantations of *Rhododendron* species and cultivars, there are few cultivars of Irish origin. The Slieve Donard Nursery, Newcastle, County Down, raised and named about seven, including 'Evelyn Slinger' (see Plate 33), during the 1960s and early 1970s before it ceased trading. An occasional cultivar has been produced from other gardens: 'Lady Dunleath' was raised at Ballywalter in County Down, 'Irish Beauty' (probably extinct) came from the Botanic Gardens in Glasnevin, 'Thomas Bolas' and 'Nigel Marshall' are both from Mount Stewart in County Down. *R. arboreum* Sm. 'Fernhill Silver' is a selected form from Fernhill in County Dublin (see below). Perhaps the most productive garden was Headfort, the demesne of the Marquis of Headfort, near Kells in County Meath. Lord Headfort raised a number of hybrids, including 'Redstart' (a dwarf, red-flowered plant, *R. aperantum* Balf. f. & Ward × *R. euchaites* Balf. f. & Forr.), 'Sangreal' (also red-flowered, a cross between *R. griersonianum* Balf. f. & Forr. and *R. venator* Tagg.), 'Kenlis' (*R. meddianum* Forr. × *R. orbiculare* Decne.) and 'Vanguard'.

'Vanguard' was the progeny of a cross between *R. venator* and *R. griersonianum* and it was raised at Headfort in the 1940s. It was described as a 'neat, rounded shrub, about 3 or 4 feet [*c.* 1 m] tall and as much across... with loose trusses of waxy, dazzling scarlet'.

The Earl of Leitrim, who owned a house and estate at Mulroy in the north of County Donegal, was another of the coterie of gardeners who admired rhododendrons and he assembled a collection in his garden. From these plants he propagated by cuttings and by seed, and for a short time in the 1940s and 1950s the Leitrim estate ran a small nursery selling shrubs, especially rhododendrons. In a catalogue published in 1950, a plant was listed as "New Hybrid (Vanguard × Thomsonii Grandiflorum)".

Three plants of this new hybrid were acquired by Henry P. McIlhenny and he planted them in his garden which was then being formed at Glenveagh Castle, about 20 km inland to the southwest of Mulroy. These three shrubs still thrive at Glenveagh, which is now owned by the state and forms part of the Glenveagh National Park. They differ slightly from each other, suggesting that what Lord Leitrim offered as a 'new hybrid' was a batch of seedlings, and not a clone selected from the batch and then propagated vegetatively. One of these seedlings was selected for propagation and distribution by Mary Forrest, until 1986 head gardener at Glenveagh Castle, and it has been named 'Mulroy Vanguard', a name which reflects the plant's origins.

'Mulroy Vanguard' forms a tall shrub – the original plant is now about 3 m high. It produces elliptical leaves, 13 cm long by 6 cm broad; they are mid-green above, paler beneath. The petiole is glabrous, about 1 cm long. The shrub flowers from April into June; the trusses are composed of about ten blossoms. Each flower has an irregular dark-red calyx and a red, bell-shaped, five-lobe corolla that is broader than long (5 cm long × 6 cm diameter); the upper three lobes of the corolla are distinctly speckled. At the base of the corolla inside are five dark nectar pouches. The ten curved stamens possess red filaments and are topped by black anthers. The arcuate style is also red.

Like most rhododendrons, this cultivar only thrives in peaty or acid soil. It must be propagated vegetatively.

'Mulroy Vanguard' was registered in 1985. When the name *R. arboreum* Sm. 'Fernhill' (AIF I: Plate 34) was put forward for registration, it was discovered that it could not be accepted, as the name 'Fernhill' was already registered; thus the name has been altered to 'Fernhill Silver'. The cultivar was registered by Mrs S. Walker and Robert Walker in 1985.

32 Cultivated by the late H. P. McIlhenny, Glenveagh Castle, County Donegal, 18 May 1985. [×0.6]

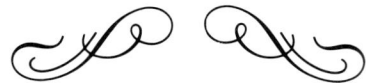

PLATE 33

Rhododendron 'Evelyn Slinger'

PLATE 33
Rhododendron 'Evelyn Slinger'

Ericaceae

Ireland has been more than fortunate in the nurserymen who in past years have plied their trade here. Of the nurseries that are now extinct, one stands pre-eminent – Slieve Donard Nursery, which took its name from the mountain at whose base it was established, outside Newcastle in County Down. Many other plants from 'The Donard' could have been selected and figured in this pair of volumes, but in restricting the portrayal of plants from Newcastle we have deliberately tried to choose the most remarkable and the best.

Mahonia × *media* Brickell 'Charity' (AIF I: Plate 31) and *Pittosporum tenuifolium* Gaertn. 'Silver Queen' (AIF I: Plate 30) represented the Slieve Donard Nursery in the original *Irish Florilegium*, as did the introductions which arose in other places – *Meconopsis* × *sheldonii* G. Taylor 'Slieve Donard' (AIF I: Plate 29), *Forsythia* × *intermedia* Zab. 'Lynwood' (AIF I: Plate 28) and *Chaenomeles* × *superba* (Frahm) Rehd. 'Rowallane' (AIF I: Plate 27). In this volume, Donard introductions are *Primula* 'Rowallane Rose' (Plate 40) and *Hypericum* 'Rowallane' (Plate 41). This cultivar of *Rhododendron* was one of a group raised at the Slieve Donard Nursery in its latter decades, and it was introduced in the autumn of 1974 in the last catalogue issued by this sadly missed nursery.

The Slieve Donard Nursery raised an unknown number of seedling rhododendrons, and from these were selected seven cultivars which were named in the published catalogues. However, none of the cultivars was registered with the International Registration Authority, which for *Rhododendron* is the Royal Horticultural Society, London, and thus the names were technically invalid. In 1986 and 1987, the cultivars were registered by Dr E. C. Nelson because they are being propagated in Northern Ireland by Carrigdale Nursery, Newcastle. Due to the rules of nomenclature, the registered names differ slightly from those published in the original catalogues. This plant, for example, was given the name 'Evelyn' when first released, but it has had to be revised to 'Evelyn Slinger' in order to comply with registration regulations.

'Evelyn Slinger' is one of the many cultivars of *Rhododendron* raised in Europe during the last quarter of a century from the Japanese dwarf species *R. yakusimanum* Nakai. It forms a low, spreading shrub reaching perhaps 1.5 m high and over 1.5 m in diameter. The young shoots have a pale-green bark and the foliage is also light green in colour. The leaves are elliptical to obovate, 10 cm by 3.5 cm, with slightly recurved margins; the lower side is sparsely clothed in a felty indumentum, but this is not dense enough to conceal the veins. There are about eight blooms in each inflorescence; the inflorescence scales are covered with short hairs. Each flower is held on a hirsute stalk about 2 cm long.

The individual flowers of 'Evelyn Slinger' have a remarkable colour and form. The most noticeable feature is the petaloid calyx, which gives the flowers an especially full appearance. In most species and cultivars of *Rhododendron*, the calyx is green or almost absent; in very few is there a petaloid calyx. In 'Evelyn Slinger', the calyx is the same colour as the corolla, salmon-pink shading to creamy-pink and red. It is irregularly campanulate with deeply cut asymmetrical lobes and may be split to the base. Slightly shorter than the corolla, it is about 3.5 cm in depth. The corolla, inside the calyx, is campanulate, 4 cm deep and about 6 cm in diameter. The five lobes (2 cm deep and 2.5 cm wide) are rounded and overlapping with crumpled, undulating margins. At the base of the corolla, inside, are five nectar pouches. The stamens are straight, about 2 cm long, with hirsute filaments and dark-red anthers. The style just emerges from the corolla; it is 3.5 cm long, straight but slightly upturned at the apex with a red-brown stigma. The ovary, 1 cm long, is green and covered in short, woolly hairs.

'Evelyn Slinger' was named after one of Leslie and Ruby Slinger's three daughters. Two other *Rhododendron* cultivars bear the names of her sisters: 'Rosealind Slinger' (with rose-pink flowers and excellent bronze young foliage) and 'Joan Slinger' (another *R. yakusimanum* hybrid with white and pink flowers and straw-coloured young leaves).

33 Cultivated by J. Murray, Dundrum, County Down, 11 June 1986. [×0.65]

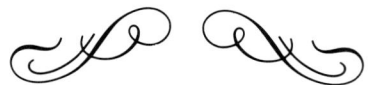

PLATE 34

Cytisus 'Lady Moore' and 'Killiney Red'

PLATE 34
Cytisus 'Lady Moore' and 'Killiney Red'

Papilionaceae   broom

Broom is a native plant in Ireland. The wild plant (*Cytisus scoparius* (L.) Link) with brilliant-yellow pea-flowers is frequently seen along road verges, and in some coastal habitats prostrate variants are occasionally found. The individual flowers are borne on almost bare stems; small, trifoliate leaves are produced after flowering in the summer. In the wild, this species does not vary substantially in flower colour, but a cultivar named 'Andreanus' with brownish-crimson wings was discovered in Normandy, France, in 1884 and it was used, for example by Daisy Hill Nursery, Newry, to create a new series of highly coloured brooms – 'Firefly' was one of the first Newry cultivars. Other species of *Cytisus* were later involved in breeding, so that nowadays in gardens, flowers with varying amounts of red are commonplace.

One of the major Irish nurseries during the present century was Watson's Nurseries of Killiney, County Dublin, and that family made brooms one of its specialities. Numerous seedlings were raised at Killiney and the Watsons selected some of the best for naming and introduction into commerce, including the two cultivars depicted here. Several of the Watson cultivars were given awards by the Royal Horticultural Society of London when exhibited at shows.

'Lady Moore', named after Phylis Moore, wife of Sir Frederick Moore, obtained an Award of Merit at Chelsea Show in 1928; in their catalogue for 1929–1930 this cultivar was described thus: 'Amongst the lovely new range of hardy brooms raised by us at Killiney this takes a prominent place. The flowers ... are exceptionally large, the wings and keel being of greater length than in any of the other varieties. This greatly enhances the effect, the wings being of a rich fiery red, the standard yellowish buff with rosy tinted reverse. The flowers are beautifully arranged along gracefully arched stems.'

It is now difficult to find plants of this cultivar, but it did survive in the National Botanic Gardens, Glasnevin, where Sir Frederick Moore was Keeper between 1879 and 1922. 'Lady Moore' grows as described, with arching stems and large flowers. It is tolerant of lime and thrives in most soils without any special care or attention. Propagation must be by cuttings, which are best taken in late summer. If seed is gathered and sown, the resulting seedlings will not be identical with the parent.

'Killiney Red' is one of the best known of the Watson brooms. It was introduced in the nursery's latter decades, but never received any award. Of shorter stature – the cultivar was described as growing low and wide with a potential height of about 1 m – 'Killiney Red' has a deep velvety-red standard, pale pink inside, with keel and wings of a similar colour. It should also be propagated only from cuttings.

Watson's Nurseries did not carry out as much plant breeding and selection as the Slieve Donard Nursery of Newcastle. However, the cultivars of *Cytisus* did achieve considerable distinction for Watson's. The firm also selected and introduced a series of cultivars of *Chamaecyparis lawsoniana* Parl. ('Killiney', 'Killiney Gold', 'Kilbogget Gold'), and was responsible for the commercial introduction of *Eucryphia* × *nymansensis* Bausch 'Mount Usher' (AIF I: Plate 22) and *Campanula garganica* Ten. 'W. H. Paine', both of which originated in private gardens. Throughout the Dublin region the nursery was renowned for the excellence of its plants, especially fruit trees, shrubs and rose cultivars. Having been established by William Watson, a native of Lanarkshire, Scotland, in 1856, the nursery ceased trading in 1966.

Because brooms are so easy to raise from seed, few of the cultivars raised by Watson's Nurseries now survive in gardens, at least as authentically labelled plants. An appeal made in 1985 for genuine material of 'Killiney Red' resulted in numerous reports of brooms purchased in Watson's Nurseries before closure, but few of the plants could be given names with certainty. Fortunately, a plant of 'Killiney Red' was growing in the garden of Michael O'Connor, Mount Merrion, and it could be authenticated, as its history was known.

34 'Lady Moore' cultivated by Dr E. C. Nelson, Celbridge, County Kildare, 27 May 1985; 'Killiney Red' (lower right) cultivated by M. O'Connor, Mount Merrion, County Dublin, 1 June 1985. [×0.8]

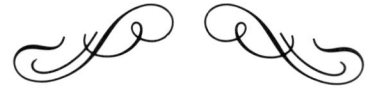

PLATE 35
Hebe 'Headfortii'

PLATE 35
Hebe 'Headfortii'

Scrophulariaceae

There exists in the southern hemisphere a group of plants which resemble woody speedwells, and indeed for most of the nineteenth century they were classified as species of *Veronica*. However, in 1921, F. W. Pennell separated these shrubby plants from the herbaceous speedwells and readopted the name *Hebe* which had been proposed for these plants by Philibert Commerson in the late 1700s – it is named after the Greek goddess of youth. While the majority of species are native in New Zealand and its off-lying islands, the genus also occurs in Australia, New Guinea, South America and the Falkland Islands, whence came the first species cultivated in Europe (*H. elliptica* (Forst. f.) Pennell).

The current *Flora of New Zealand* recognizes eighty species of *Hebe*, but it is a difficult genus to classify, as the species hybridize both in the wild and in gardens. Most of the New Zealand species are cultivated in Europe and over forty are listed from Irish gardens. Many more cultivars and plants of unknown and uncertain parentage are also grown; some are elegant and beautiful, but others are unexciting and weedy.

Hebe 'Headfortii' is one of the finest of the cultivars available to gardeners in Ireland. It is tender and is sometimes killed by severe frosts, but generally a small amount of protection – for example, covering the plants with yew branches in winter – will ensure that it survives. All of the species and cultivars appear to be tolerant of lime-rich soil and they are especially useful in coastal gardens, as they can also tolerate salt-laden winds.

Hebe 'Headfortii' was raised by the Marquis of Headfort in his garden at Kells, County Meath. He had obtained seed from New Zealand, but the source or exact provenance of the seed is not known. Lord Headfort recognized the merits of this plant, and by 1930 it was being distributed under the name "*Veronica headfortii*". The Headfort *Hebe* is not known in the wild in New Zealand and it is more than likely that it is a hybrid, but its parentage is also mysterious. The present edition of W. J. Bean's *Trees and shrubs hardy in the British Isles* places it near *H. macrocarpa* (Vahl) Cockayne & Allan, but that is at best a guess, and it does not resemble that species in certain critical characteristics.

The cultivar forms a low, rounded shrub, usually reaching about 75 cm in height, but in very sheltered gardens it may be over 1 m. The leaves are evergreen, elliptical or ovate, to 4 cm long and about 1.5 cm broad; they are dark, glossy green and are arranged in opposite pairs on the stems. The leaf-bud which terminates every stem is elliptical and has a conspicuous sinus – a critical character in identifying *Hebe* taxa. The flowers are grouped in axillary, elongated racemes, each composed of about fifty separate blossoms. The individual flower has a red-brown calyx, four rich purple-blue petals fused at the base into a short corolla tube which is white inside. There are two stamens with long, purple filaments, and a shorter reflexed style. *Hebe* 'Headfortii' flowers in late winter if it is mild, sometimes as early as February; otherwise it comes into bloom in the spring and continues through the early summer.

This shrub should only be propagated by cuttings taken in summer when the young wood is ripening; like other cultivars and species of *Hebe*, even small cuttings will root very easily. It will grow in any type of soil but it does require protection if it is planted in areas where frosts are frequent.

Hebe 'Headfortii' is one of a group of cultivars produced by the Marquis of Headfort in the first half of this century. He was one of that coterie of great gardeners, including Sir Frederick Moore of Glasnevin, Hugh Armytage Moore of Rowallane and Edward Walpole of Mount Usher, which took a special interest in growing the best, new introductions, and the demesne of Kells was richly planted with rare plants. Lord Headfort was particularly interested in *Rhododendron* species and cultivars, raising numerous hybrids from his own seed (see Plate 32).

35 Cultivated in the National Botanic Gardens, Glasnevin, Dublin, 3 June 1985. [×0.8]

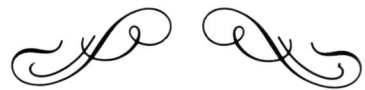

PLATE 36

Nerine 'Glensavage Gem' and 'John Fanning'

PLATE 36
Nerine 'Glensavage Gem' and 'John Fanning'

Amaryllidaceae — Guernsey lily

The genus *Nerine* is composed of about thirty species, all of which are native in southern Africa. For more than three centuries these bulbs have been cultivated in Europe, and the famous Guernsey lily (*N. sarniensis* (L.) Herbert), said to have reached the island aboard a ship that was wrecked on its rocky shores, is one of those plants whose botanical and vernacular names are most inappropriate – it is not a native plant there.

As they are easy to grow indoors – they require no special treatment and actually thrive on neglect – cultivars of *Nerine* are popular. Numerous hybrids have been raised.

Several hundred seedlings were produced in the Botanic Gardens, Glasnevin, during the last two decades of the nineteenth century and in the first thirty years of the present century. Over one hundred cultivars were named, usually after lady gardeners, but on one frosty night in 1930 the entire collection was killed. Since then the National Botanic Gardens has not undertaken any breeding work on *Nerine* and does not hold a collection of these plants now.

The Irish tradition of breeding *Nerine* dates back to William Edward Gumbleton, who raised and selected several cultivars in the 1880s. In more recent years, the genus was the particular interest of Miss Doris Findlater, and the two cultivars depicted were raised by her. 'John Fanning' bears the name of the late Assistant Keeper of the National Botanic Gardens, Glasnevin, and 'Glensavage Gem' was named after the house in which Miss Findlater and her sister lived at Blackrock, County Dublin.

Nerine 'Glensavage Gem' has been exhibited on at least one occasion by Tony Norris, and he was awarded a Preliminary Cultural Certificate by the Royal Horticultural Society of London for the cultivar in 1968. 'Glensavage Gem' is a seedling resulting from a deliberate cross effected in 1959 between a good form of *N. bowdenii* Watson and a cultivar named 'Cortusa'; the latter plant was the seed parent. The seedling flowered for the first time in 1964. It has tall stems, up to 1 m in height, bearing a truss of scarlet flowers. Each flower is composed of six perianth segments, 6 cm long and less than 1 cm broad, with distinctly crisped margins; in certain lights, the flowers glisten as if spattered with gold dust. Tony Norris considers that 'Glensavage Gem' is one of the finest cultivars currently available, although it has not been widely distributed and is extremely rare in cultivation.

Nerine 'John Fanning' has never been released commercially, but Doris Findlater did distribute bulbs to friends, including Tony Norris, Miss Rita Rutherfoord, and to the National Botanic Gardens, Glasnevin. This is also a robust, tall plant, with a fine truss of claret-rose flowers. One particular characteristic of 'John Fanning' is that the perianth acquires a distinctive purple tint as the flowers mature, and especially as they begin to wither.

Both of these cultivars are deciduous, flowering before the leaves appear. They require no water when resting and should never be given fertilizers; in their native habitats, *Nerine* species grow in impoverished soils and such conditions must be imitated in cultivation to ensure that the bulbs will bloom. The flowering spike begins to emerge about the beginning of September and the flowers are fully developed by the middle of October. The blooms of *Nerine* last for many weeks if kept relatively cool, and given their undemanding habits, these bulbs make excellent house plants.

Doris Findlater (1895–1981) was educated at Alexandra College, Dublin, where she attended classes in botany and horticulture given by Canon F. C. Hayes. She developed a keen interest in gardening and served for many years on the council of the Royal Horticultural Society of Ireland; she was chairman of the council in 1966 and was elected an honorary member of the RHSI in 1975. She was always fond of roses and Dicksons of Hawlmark (see Plate 48) named one after her. Doris Findlater raised a suite of *Nerine* cultivars, most of which are extant in private collections. The named ones include 'Guy Fawkes', 'The Spider', 'The Giraffe', 'Silchester Rose', 'Tweedledum' and 'Tweedledee'. She also took an interest in breeding daffodils, but none of her bulbs was of sufficient merit to introduce and name. In the 1970s, she found a remarkable

continued on page 160

36 'Glensavage Gem' (upper specimen) cultivated by Miss Sheila Findlater, Glenageary, County Dublin, 18 October 1985. 'John Fanning' (two lower specimens) cultivated by Miss Rita Rutherfoord, Enniskerry, County Wicklow, 20 October 1985. [×0.6]

continued

erect-flowered form of *Daboecia cantabrica* (Huds.) Koch (AIF I: Plate 17), which has recently been propagated and named after her (*D. cantabrica* f. *blumii* McClintock 'Doris Findlater').

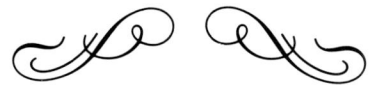

PLATE 37
Anthemis 'Grallagh Gold'

PLATE 37
Anthemis 'Grallagh Gold'

Asteraceae

Anthemis species are native in Europe and western Asia; the genus contains about two hundred species, several of which are widely cultivated in gardens. *A. sancti-johannis* Turrill from Bulgaria and *A. tinctoria* L., which is more wide-ranging in Europe and the Near East, are believed to be the parents of the cultivar 'Grallagh Gold'.

Anthemis 'Grallagh Gold' is a short-lived perennial herb. It has deeply divided, silvery-green leaves, up to 7 cm long and about 4 cm broad. The individual blooms, like those of all members of the Asteraceae (Compositae), are complex inflorescences composed of numerous minute florets. The outer, or ray, florets have long, strap-shaped corollas which resemble a single petal but are formed from five fused petals. The inner disc florets do not have the elongated corolla, but possess five smaller petals fused into a tube. The ray florets in this plant are bright golden-yellow, about 5 cm long and 0.7 cm broad. The whole flowering head forms a brilliant-yellow daisy 10 cm in diameter.

This plant is of outstanding merit. It blossoms for many weeks; usually, the peak of flowering occurs during late July and early August. The blooms last for three weeks when cut, and are larger than those of most other cultivars of *Anthemis*.

Being a short-lived and slightly tender plant, it is advisable to take cuttings every year; shoots, dipped in a rooting hormone and inserted into a sandy compost, will develop roots within a few weeks. Cuttings taken early in the year (about May) will flower in late summer. Cuttings should also be taken in the autumn and over-wintered indoors in frost-prone areas to ensure that the cultivar survives. However, well-established plants will usually survive without protection out-of-doors, except in the most severe winters. 'Grallagh Gold' tends to become unshapely and woody after two years and propagation is also advisable to ensure that young plants are always available.

This cultivar, and its rarer counterpart 'Beauty of Grallagh', were chance seedlings that arose before 1948 in the garden of Miss Blanche Poë (1876–1968) at Nenagh, County Tipperary – they both bear the name of her house. 'Grallagh Gold' was exhibited at the council of the Royal Horticultural Society of Ireland on 9 July 1948 and Miss Poë was awarded a First Class Certificate for this new plant. In the same year, it was introduced into commerce by Perry's Hardy Plant Farm of Enfield in Middlesex; Miss Poë gave Reginald Perry exclusive rights to sell the cultivar outside the Republic of Ireland. 'Grallagh Gold' also obtained an Award of Merit from the Royal Dutch Horticultural Society. It is not common in gardens now and is rarely sold in nurseries and garden centres, although it is easy to propagate.

Anthemis 'Beauty of Grallagh' (originally named 'Grallagh Glory') was introduced in 1951, also by Perry's Hardy Plant Farm. Again, Miss Poë gave Reginald Perry exclusive rights to market the cultivar. It is not as sturdy as 'Grallagh Gold' and has deeper golden-orange flowers. 'Beauty of Grallagh' is now very rare in gardens and is in danger of becoming extinct.

Miss Poë's father is commemorated in the double-flowered snowdrop, *Galanthus* 'Hill Poë' (AIF I: Plate 36). Her uncle, John Bennett-Poë, was a renowned horticulturist who had a particular interest in *Nerine* and was a close friend of William Edward Gumbleton (see Plates 31 and 36).

37 Cultivated by Mrs W. F. Walsh, Lusk, County Dublin, 12 August 1985. [×0.6]

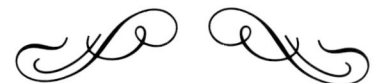

PLATE 38

Sambucus nigra Linnaeus

f. *porphyrophylla* E. C. Nelson

'Guincho Purple'

PLATE 38
Sambucus nigra Linnaeus
f. *porphyrophylla* E. C. Nelson
'Guincho Purple'

Caprifoliaceae   elder

The elder is a common hedgerow plant throughout Ireland, but especially in areas where the soil is a heavy, lime-rich clay. Ground that has been distributed and then left to return to the wild is often colonized by elder, which has a tendency to be a weedy shrub.

There are several forms of elder cultivated in gardens; the commonest is the cut- or parsley-leaved elder (*Sambucus nigra* f. *laciniata* (L.) Zab.), which has finely dissected leaves. This has been collected in Ireland on several occasions, and was cultivated here in the late seventeenth century by Sir Arthur Rawdon at Moira, County Down. Cultivars with white ('Albovariegata') or yellow ('Aureomarginata') marginal variegation on the leaflets are also available to gardeners, as is a golden-foliaged one ('Aurea'). Other variants include plants with green fruits, and plants with pink flowers.

The cultivar depicted here has purple foliage and pink flowers; it has been listed under the names 'Foliis Purpureis' and 'Purpureus' but these are invalid under the International Code of Nomenclature of Cultivated Plants. The fancy name 'Guincho Purple' is published here for the clone propagated from the late Mrs Vera Mackie's garden, Guincho at Helen's Bay in County Down. This is the clone for which Hillier Nurseries gained an Award of Merit from the Royal Horticultural Society of London in 1977.

Sambucus nigra 'Guincho Purple' forms a tall, bushy shrub, or even a small tree; the original plant still grows at Guincho and is now over 5 m in height. Like the green-leaved form, this cultivar produces vigorous, straight shoots from the base, but the older branches may be pendulous. The young foliage is green, but it rapidly turns dark purple and then fades slightly as it matures, becoming metallic, bronzy purple; some leaves may display flashes of bright green, 'as if someone had drawn a paintbrush across them'. The leaves are pinnately compound, generally with five or seven elliptical leaflets; when fully expanded, the leaves can be 15 to 20 cm long and the leaflets about 7.5 cm long. The inflorescence is flat and umbrella-like with five principal segments. The individual flowers are small (about 0.5 cm across) and very numerous; they are composed of five orbicular petals (*c.* 0.2 cm across) alternating with five pink stamens. In bud, the flowers are purple-pink; the outer side of the petals remains that colour but the inner surface is creamy white. The fruits, like those of the green-leaved elder, are black and juicy berries.

'Guincho Purple' was originally found in Scotland by Mrs Mackie about 1957 when she was on holiday. She took cuttings and rooted one, which she planted at Guincho. In October 1969, Harold Hillier saw the purple-leaved elder when he was visiting Northern Ireland and he obtained cuttings from Mrs Mackie. Hillier Nurseries propagated the clone and exhibited it under the invalid name *S. nigra* 'Purpurea'.

Purple-leaved elders are not recorded in older botanical and horticultural books, although some of the other forms and varieties have been known for many centuries. The first published account of this variant appeared in 1964, when R. D. Meikle recorded that Robert Howat had found two plants between Forcett and Richmond (Yorkshire) in the north of England. Mr Howat presented plants to the Royal Botanic Gardens, Kew, and later to the Royal Horticultural Society's Garden, Wisley. Another plant was discovered elsewhere in Britain some years ago, but precise details are not recorded. The plants raised from Robert Howat's discovery are indistinguishable from the Guincho clone, and while it does not have a cultivar name, may be referred to *S. nigra* f. *porphyrophylla*.

38 Cultivated in National Botanic Gardens, Glasnevin, Dublin (from Guincho, County Down), 10 June 1985. [×0.7]

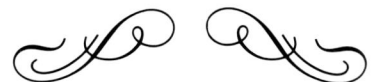

PLATE 39

Bergenia 'Ballawley'

PLATE 39
Bergenia 'Ballawley'

Saxifragaceae

These large-leaved members of the Saxifragaceae have had several generic names during the past two centuries. While today there is some stability in their nomenclature, they were listed formerly under *Megascea* and *Saxifraga*. The present generic name *Bergenia* commemorates Karl August von Bergen (1704–1768).

Bergenia contains perhaps six species that inhabit the Himalaya, China and northeastern Asia. At least five are in cultivation in Europe, and over the last century many interspecific hybrids have been raised. One of the first nurserymen to undertake breeding work was Thomas Smith, founder of the Daisy Hill Nursery, Newry, County Down. While still working with Rodger, McLelland and Sons, Daisy Hill's predecessor, Smith raised a hybrid between *B. purpurascens* (Hook. f. & Thoms.) Engl. and *B. cordifolia* (Haw.) Sternberg; it had large, flared flowers and was named *B.* × *smithii* Engl. & Irmscher. In its original form, it seems now to be extinct. During the last decade of the nineteenth century, Smith produced and named about twenty-five other cultivars, but few of them can be recognized and named today. 'Distinction' and 'Profusion' are in cultivation still and have recently been returned to Daisy Hill Nursery for propagation.

The cultivar 'Ballawley' is of more recent origin. It was a seedling raised at Ballawley Park, Dundrum, County Dublin, by Desmond Shaw-Smith. The plant must have originated in the late 1930s, since it was exhibited on 29 March 1944 at a show of the Royal Horticultural Society of Ireland, and on that occasion the cultivar received a First Class Certificate. Other awards followed; the Royal Horticultural Society of London gave it an Award of Merit in 1955 and in 1965 an Award of Garden Merit.

Bergenia 'Ballawley' is a remarkably fine garden plant. It has large, leathery leaves which are bright grass-green when young; as they age, the leaves turn darker, glossy green and the reverse becomes red. In winter, they turn a most beautiful crimson. The largest leaves on healthy plants may be 50 cm long and as much wide; they are orbicular or ovate in outline with toothed margins. The flowers are borne in a lax inflorescence atop an erect stem which is at least 50 cm high. The inflorescence is branched and the branches and the calyx are tinged with crimson. The individual flowers are nodding, their petals are rich purple, obovate and up to 1.7 cm long and about 1.2 cm broad.

This plant flowers in April and May, when the contrast between the brilliant-green young leaves and the rich-purple and crimson inflorescence is most striking. *Bergenia* 'Ballawley' thrives in a rich loam, and is tolerant of lime; for the very best results, the plants should be liberally mulched with compost or given regular foliar feeds. When flourishing, this cultivar serves as an excellent ground-cover.

Bergenia 'Ballawley' was originally called 'Delbees', a name taken from the plant's putative parents; one was called *B. delavayi* (Franch.) Engl. (now correctly *B. purpurascens* (Hook. f. & Thoms.) Engl.), and the other was called *B. beesiana*, which is an invalid synonym for the same species.

Ballawley was Desmond Shaw-Smith's family home and it contained a fine rock-garden. The nursery was established in the 1920s and it was essentially stocked with surplus plants from the garden. However, several active breeding and selection programmes undertaken by Desmond Shaw-Smith resulted in fine garden plants. *Aubrieta* was a particular favourite, and a number of cultivars were introduced, including 'Ballawley Giant', 'Amethyst' and 'Pink Parakeet'; none of these is known to have survived. In 1941, he introduced *Saxifraga* 'Ballawley Guardsman', a mossy saxifrage with deep-red flowers; it is still one of the best of Shaw-Smith's introductions, and like the *Bergenia* widely grown in Irish gardens. Ballawley Nursery was the first to offer for sale the beautiful red-flowered cultivar *Daboecia cantabrica* (Huds.) Koch 'Praegerae' (AIF I: Plate 17). The nursery closed about 1955.

39 Cultivated by Mrs H. Dillon, Ranelagh, Dublin, 4 May 1984. [×0.6]

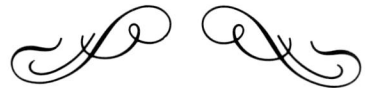

PLATE 40

Primula 'Rowallane Rose'

PLATE 40
Primula 'Rowallane Rose'

Primulaceae												candelabra primrose

Candelabra primroses take their garden name from the tiered flowers. They are familiar inhabitants of Irish gardens, especially those with extensive waterside areas and damp woodland glades, for they flourish in rich, moist soils. At Annes Grove in County Cork, Mulroy in County Donegal and Mount Stewart in County Down, the early summer would not be the same without the stately carpets of *Primula pulverulenta* Duthie, *P. japonica* Gray and the many cultivars and hybrids that are naturalized.

Irish gardens and nurseries have produced and named about thirty cultivars of the candelabra primroses. Brian Mulligan created *P.* × *chunglenta* Mulligan by crossing *P. pulverulenta* and *P. chungensis* Balf. f. & Ward. H. D. M. Barton of The Bush, Antrim, named several seedlings, but these no longer survive in cultivation. From Sir Josslyn Gore-Booth's garden and nursery at Lissadell in County Sligo came the fiery-red 'Red Hugh', a cultivar that is still available but very rare. Other Lissadell hybrids included the "Asthore Hybrids", 'Aileen Aroon', 'Lissadell Pink' and 'Molly Malone', but most of these are no longer recognized in gardens.

Possibly the finest of the Irish candelabra cultivars, and the one most widely cultivated, is 'Rowallane Rose' which was, like so many of the others, a chance seedling; this particular one occurred in the Walled Garden at Rowallane about 1935. Graham Stuart Thomas was the first to publish a reference to it when he wrote an account of Rowallane for the *Journal of the Royal Horticultural Society* in 1950. As with so many of Rowallane's manavilins, the primrose was produced commercially by the Slieve Donard Nursery, Newcastle, County Down.

'Rowallane Rose' has obscure origins; its parents are not known. It has grass-green leaves which form a rosette, out of which arises the flowering spike. The leaves are typical of the candelabra primroses, spathulate, about 15 cm long, and about 7 cm broad. The flowering stem can reach over 1 m tall in ideal conditions, with at least four whorls of flowers. The flowers in each whorl open together, the lowest whorl opening first, followed some days later by the next, and so on – flowering may extend over one month from the beginning of June. Each individual blossom, about 2 cm in diameter, is composed of five fused petals which have deeply lobed apices; they are rose-red. In the centre there is a deep golden-yellow 'eye'.

This cultivar is sterile and must be increased by division of the rosettes in late summer or in the spring. If seed ever is formed, it would not yield seedlings of the true colour; in any case, it is best to remove the flowering stems once the flowers have withered. 'Rowallane Rose' thrives in soil well mulched with leaf-mould, and is apparently tolerant of lime. It will respond well to division at least every three years.

40 Cultivated by David Shackleton, Beech Park, Clonsilla, County Dublin, 17 June 1985. [×0.7]

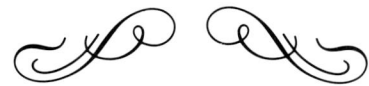

PLATE 41

Hypericum 'Rowallane'

PLATE 41
Hypericum 'Rowallane'

Hypericaceae (Guttiferae)　　　　　　　　　　　　　　　　　　　　　　　　shrubby St John's wort

Hypericum ranges through the northern hemisphere mainly in temperate regions, but one of the putative parents of this cultivar is a native in the Indonesian archipelago from the mountains of northern Sumatra eastwards into Java, Bali and Sulawesi (Celebes). Nine species are native in Ireland, all of them herbs except the common tutsan (*H. androsaemum* L.), which is a low-growing shrub. Many exotic St John's worts are cultivated in Irish gardens and their original habitats include Europe (for example, *H. calycinum* L.), North America and the Orient.

All the species and cultivars of *Hypericum* familiar to Irish botanists and gardeners have yellow flowers composed of five petals with a central boss of numerous stamens arranged in five fascicles. There is much variation in the size of the individual flowers and in their arrangement on the shoots; in some species the flowers are solitary, while in others they are arranged in clusters of varying complexity. *Hypericum* species always have leaves in opposite pairs, and the size of the leaves differs from species to species.

The cultivar 'Rowallane' bears the name of one of Ireland's finest gardens, famed for its collection of rhododendrons, for its natural rock-garden, and as the home of a quartet of excellent cultivars. As well as *Hypericum* 'Rowallane', the garden has yielded *Primula* 'Rowallane Rose' (see Plate 40), *Viburnum plicatum* Thunb. f. *tomentosum* (Thunb.) Rehd. 'Rowallane', and *Chaenomeles* × *superba* Frahm 'Rowallane' (AIF I: Plate 27). There are several other cultivars, some only recently named, which also had their origins in Rowallane, but they are not yet well known and widely distributed; these include cultivars of *Tanacetum parthenium* (L.) Schultz, *Pieris formosa* D. Don and *Crocosmia masonorum* (Bolus) Brown.

Hypericum 'Rowallane' was a chance seedling in the garden. It was spotted about 1932 by Hugh Armytage Moore, the owner of Rowallane. He was friendly with the Slinger family who owned the Slieve Donard Nursery in the town of Newcastle near Rowallane, and that nursery propagated and introduced the cultivar in the early 1940s. In 1943, when shown by Slieve Donard Nursery, *Hypericum* 'Rowallane' gained an Award of Merit from the Royal Horticultural Society of London.

The precise parentage of the cultivar is not known, but it is suggested that one of the parents was the Indonesian species *H. leschenaultii* Choisy, which is hardy in the milder parts of Ireland and Britain. It is a montane species, growing in open woodland and on grassy slopes above 1500 m altitude. Having been cultivated in Europe since about 1882, this shrub was growing in Rowallane about the time when this cultivar arose; it is still cultivated in a few gardens today and is listed for Mount Stewart, County Down.

The other parent was probably *H. hookerianum* Wight & Arnott, and particularly the cultivar named 'Charles Rogers' (formerly known as *H. hookerianum* 'Rogersii'), which came from central Burma and was introduced by Charles Rogers, the Chief Conservator of Forests in Burma and a friend of Lady Charlotte Wheeler-Cuffe (see AIF I: Plate 47).

Hypericum 'Rowallane' is not fully hardy. Severe frost or prolonged east winds can damage its shoots and may even kill plants to the ground. 'Rowallane' should be planted in a sheltered place and it will flourish best in the milder areas. If not affected by cold, shrubs reach 2 m in height, forming long, arching stems. The leaves, which are usually deciduous in Ireland, are elliptical, about 7.5 cm long and 3 cm broad, glabrous, dark green on the upper surface and paler beneath. The flowers are borne at the tips of the main stems and side shoots either in groups of three or singly and, depending on the season, they open from June onwards – the peak flowering period here is usually August and September. The individual blooms, deep golden yellow, are formed like a shallow cup about 7 cm in diameter. Each of the petals is obovate with a slightly crinkled margin but lacking the glands sometimes seen in *Hypericum* flowers. Each stamen fascicle contains as many as ninety individual stamens, and these are also golden yellow. The central capsule is ovoid, about 1 cm long,

continued on page 180

41 Cultivated by Mrs W. F. Walsh, Lusk, County Dublin, 22 August 1984. [×0.7]

continued

crowned with five curved styles. This cultivar is sterile, so no seeds are produced.

Plants must be raised from cuttings taken in the late summer when the wood is hardening. 'Rowallane' will tolerate a lime-rich soil, and it is readily available from the better nurseries and garden centres.

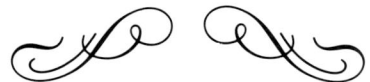

PLATE 42

Ilex × altaclerensis (Loudon) Dallimore

'Hendersonii' and 'Lawsoniana'

PLATE 42
Ilex × *altaclerensis* (Loudon) Dallimore
'Hendersonii' and 'Lawsoniana'

Aquifoliaceae   holly, cuilean

Ilex aquifolium L., the holly, is a native plant in Ireland and is especially abundant in the milder areas of the west and south. It is one of the principal understorey shrubs in the native oak woodlands of the southwest, and is a common hedgerow tree in those regions too. Its dark, evergreen leaves, armed with marginal spines, and its red berries are familiar to all as Christmas decorations. However, the holly was a highly valued and sacred plant long before Ireland was converted to Christianity, and it was protected under the ancient Brehon Laws.

An important characteristic of holly is that it is dioecious – the individual plants bear unisexual flowers; male plants never produce berries, which can only be borne by the females, but it is essential to have male and female plants growing together for fruit to form.

There are at least four hundred different species of *Ilex* distributed throughout the world in both temperate and tropical regions. Only one is native in Ireland, but over twenty are cultivated in Irish gardens, including the Chinese species *I. pernyi* Franch., which Dr Augustine Henry (see Plates 19 and 28) collected in central China during the late 1880s.

The native holly has sported many cultivars and some of these – for example, the multi-spined hedgehog holly ('Ferox') and the variegated ones – were certainly cultivated in Irish gardens during the seventeenth and eighteenth centuries. *I. perado* Aiton, which grows on the Atlantic island of Madeira, was probably the first exotic species introduced to Ireland; it was cultivated out-of-doors in the College Botanic Garden, Dublin, before 1825 and must have been grown in other Irish gardens during the latter part of the eighteenth century.

Ilex aquifolium and *I. perado* hybridize readily when planted in close proximity, and the progeny of this cross is named *I.* × *altaclerensis* (Loudon) Dallimore. The hybrid was first raised after 1760, which is the year *I. perado* was introduced into cultivation in Britain. In 1838, John Claudius Loudon gave it the name *I.* × *altaclerensis* after Highclere (in Latin *Alta Clera*), the estate of the earls of Carnarvon near Newbury in Berkshire, where the hybrid was said to have originated.

It was, however, also raised in Ireland. Edward Hodgins, who owned a nursery near Dunganstown in County Wicklow between about 1780 and 1820, raised hollies from seed and two of his seedlings have been recognized as *I.* × *altaclerensis*. They were widely distributed to gardeners and other nurseries during the early decades of the nineteenth century and have become popular evergreen shrubs. Over the years, however, their names have been muddled and confused.

One of Hodgins's seedlings was a male plant, and it is correctly named *I.* × *altaclerensis* 'Hodginsii'; it has also been labelled 'Shepherdii' after John Shepherd, one-time curator of Liverpool Botanic Garden.

The second plant was female, and its correct name is *I.* × *altaclerensis* 'Hendersonii', but to confuse matters, it was distributed under the name 'Hodginsii' during the mid-1800s at least. 'Hendersonii' is a robust holly; old, mature plants have been recorded as reaching about 14 m in height. The stems and leaf-stalks are green but lightly flushed with purple ('Hodginsii' has dark-purple stems). The leaves are dull, dark green above and paler beneath; they are ovate, up to 12 cm long and about 6 cm broad. Some of the leaves are entirely without spines, but others have a few small spines near the apex. The small flowers, borne in the early spring, are tinged with purple when in bud and open to white; each flower is about 0.5 cm across and composed of four petals and a central pistil. This cultivar produces a good crop of large, brownish-red berries.

Edward Hodgins was one of the few Irish nurserymen who supplied plants for the newly established Botanic Gardens at Glasnevin after 1795. Little else is known about him. He died in the early 1800s, for by 1837 the proprietor of the Dunganstown Nursery is listed as Robert Hodgins, perhaps Edward's son. Edward Hodgins raised 'Hendersonii' in the early 1800s and

continued on page 184

42 Cultivated (both cultivars) in National Botanic Gardens, Glasnevin, 19 November 1984. [×0.55]

continued

distributed it to Messrs Lawson, a nursery company in Edinburgh, which made it commercially available about 1846. John Shepherd, the curator of Liverpool Botanic Garden, also had this holly and he sent it to Fisher and Holmes of Handsworth in Middlesex, which nursery named it 'Hendersonii' after a Mr Henderson who was a friend of John Shepherd.

The native holly sometimes sports a variegated shoot (one with marginal variegation was seen at Annaghmakerrig, County Monaghan, in December 1985), and variegated seedlings may also be found (Cormac Foley noticed one with a central flash of cream in the Killarney National Park on 31 May 1986). The hybrid with *I. perado* has also yielded variegated clones. These all originated as branch sports – no variegated hybrid seedlings have been reported. 'Hendersonii' has produced three sports: 'Golden King' (despite its name, this clone is female), 'Hendersonii Variegata' and 'Lawsoniana'.

'Lawsoniana' is an excellent garden plant, and well-grown specimens are as robust as its parent. Its leaves are as large as those of 'Hendersonii' and, like that cultivar, they are either unarmed or sparsely armed with short spines. The leaf edge is banded with dark green, but inside this irregular margin there is a central splash of gold rimmed with light greyish-green; the central gold fades somewhat as the leaf ages until it is virtually cream. As it is a female, 'Lawsoniana' does produce berries, but not as profusely as 'Hendersonii', and in any case they do not enhance the shrub's appearance.

According to a note published by William Edward Gumbleton (see Plate 46) in *The Gardeners' Chronicle* of 12 May 1888, 'Lawsoniana' originated in Mr Hodgens's nursery at Cloughjordan in County Tipperary. Hitherto I have believed that Gumbleton made an error and that he meant Edward Hodgins of Dunganstown. However, it is now clear that he was correct.

About 1836, John Hodgins came from County Wicklow to Cloughjordan and there established a nursery which, when he died, was taken over by his son William; John's relationship to Edward Hodgins of Dunganstown is not known, although it is probable that he was a younger son. William Hodgins ran the nursery until his death in 1913. A remarkable collection of documents, including seed catalogues and correspondence beginning in the 1850s, has recently come to my attention; this material represents one of the most complete archives of any Irish nursery. These papers show that the Cloughjordan nursery supplied vegetables, tree saplings and seeds to clients throughout central Ireland but there are no indications that ornamental garden plants were propagated in quantity. Thus, alas, the Hodginses' archive does not directly illuminate the problem of the history of *Ilex* 'Lawsoniana'; it merely establishes beyond doubt the existence of Hodgins's Cloughjordan nursery. Other evidence suggests that two brothers, John and Robert, were at Cloughjordan before 1836, for they contributed records of Irish native plants to J. T. Mackay's *Flora Hibernica* which was published that year.

It is therefore possible to say that either John Hodgins or his son William noticed this variegated sport and had it propagated, and also that W. E. Gumbleton was correct in ascribing 'Lawsoniana' to the Tipperary nursery (although he did confuse 'Lawsoniana' with the gold-margined sport now named 'Golden King').

Hodgins sent scions of the variant to the Lawson Nursery in Edinburgh – the holly was originally called *Ilex lawsonii* – and it was from Edinburgh that it was widely distributed. The sport was noted by Karl Koch in 1872 and appeared in trade catalogues after 1874. 'Lawsoniana' was awarded a First Class Certificate by the Royal Horticultural Society of London in 1894.

PLATE 43

Papaver 'Fireball'

(syn. *P. orientale* 'Nanum Flore Pleno')

PLATE 43
Papaver 'Fireball'
(syn. *P. orientale* 'Nanum Flore Pleno')

Papaveraceae   poppy

This small, perennial poppy has a creeping, underground rhizome – it was described by Murray Hornibrook as an 'ineradicable weed' because of its remarkable ability to spread by these far-reaching stems. It is, however, sterile and does not set seed, a characteristic which suggests that it is a hybrid.

Brian Mathew, taxonomist at the Royal Botanic Gardens, Kew, has studied *Papaver* 'Fireball' and has concluded that it is a hybrid of *P. pseudo-orientale* (Fedde) Medw. and *P. lateritium* Koch.

It is certain that 'Fireball' is not a cultivar of *P. orientale* L., as it bears leaf-like bracts on the flowering stems; in any case, Brian Mathew has pointed out that true *P. orientale* is very rare in cultivation. However, *P. pseudo-orientale*, which is closely allied to *P. orientale*, does have bracts and it is one of the most likely parent species. The other parent must have been a dwarf poppy, and Brian Mathew argues that the Turkish species *P. lateritium* is the best candidate. It is stoloniferous like 'Fireball', only grows to about 35 cm in height and has pale-green, coarsely toothed leaves, again like 'Fireball'.

Papaver 'Fireball' bears bright scarlet-red flowers early in the summer; it usually begins to bloom in the middle of May and continues into early June. The individual blossoms are borne singly on erect stems about 30 cm tall. Each flower is composed of numerous narrow petals, 3 cm long and about 0.5 cm broad. There are no stamens, and although a capsule is formed, the plant never produces seeds; the obconical capsule is green, about 1.5 cm long and about 0.4 cm in diameter. The flower-buds are encased from two deciduous calyx segments which are covered outside with coarse, whitish hairs; before the flower opens the bud droops but becomes erect as the calyx segments begin to separate. The leaves appear in March; they are narrow (up to 3 cm wide), lanceolate and covered with stiff hairs, and reach about 15 cm in length when mature.

This 'ineradicable weed' came from the garden of a house called Kellyville, near Athy in County Kildare, during the 1870s. It was most probably a chance seedling, and was noticed by Mrs Webber, who was the mother of Lady Alice Coote of Ballyfin, County Laois. Lady Coote gave her mother's dwarf poppy to Murray Hornibrook, who in turn gave it to the Dutch nurseryman, H. den Ouden of Boskoop. The poppy was named and introduced into commerce by den Ouden in the 1920s. Despite having been named 'Fireball', this cultivar acquired the name 'Nanum Flore Pleno' and is so called in various horticultural books.

Murray Hornibrook was being unfair to 'Fireball' when he described it as a weed – a weed is simply a plant growing where it is not wanted. Certainly it can be rampant, but as a ground-cover plant 'Fireball' is useful. It is easily propagated by transplanting fragments of the rhizomes and thrives in most types of soil, including heavy clay. It is most attractive when the foliage is fresh and when it is in flower. 'Fireball' is occasionally listed by nurseries, and is not uncommon in Irish gardens.

43 Cultivated by Mrs C. Fennell, Burtown House, Athy, County Kildare, 10 June 1984. [×0.6]

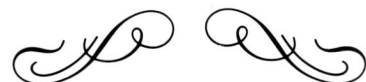

PLATE 44

Narcissus 'Foundling'

PLATE 44
Narcissus 'Foundling'

Amaryllidaceae daffodil

The breeding of daffodils has been carried out in Ireland with considerable success for over one hundred years, beginning with the work of William Baylor Hartland. Guy Wilson and Lionel Richardson were the principal enthusiasts during the first half of this century, and they produced many excellent cultivars, including 'Cantatrice' (AIF I: Plate 37) and 'Kingscourt' (AIF I: Plate 38). At the present time, Brian Duncan of Omagh, County Tyrone, is producing numerous fine bulbs and has received many medals for his cultivars. Less productive, but no less excellent, is Kate Reade of Carncairn, County Antrim, whose outstanding contribution is undoubtedly 'Foundling'.

Narcissus 'Foundling' is a relatively small daffodil; the flowering stem rarely exceeds 30 cm in height. The individual flowers are over 7 cm in diameter and have white outer perianth segments. The salmon-pink corona is 3 cm across and 1.5 cm deep; it is deeply ribbed and expands slightly near the mouth. The most noteworthy characteristic of 'Foundling' is its recurving petals, a characteristic which has led to the suggestion that this is a hybrid of *N. cyclamineus* DC.

'Foundling' was an orphan seedling; its parents are not known, its lineage cannot be recorded. While it is classified as a "Cyclamineus Narcissus" for show purposes, it is most unlikely that that diminutive species, a native of northwestern Iberia, was directly involved as a parent of 'Foundling'. It is, indeed, unnecesary to make such a suggestion, as the recurved petals could have arisen simply by a mutation in the chromosomes of these highly bred plants. Whatever its parents were, this is a dainty cultivar of considerable charm. 'Foundling' was not the first of the pink-flowered daffodils to possess recurved petals; Lionel Richardson raised one and named it 'Kelpie', but it was never introduced commercially. Perhaps 'Kelpie' was one of the antecedents of 'Foundling'.

Mrs Reade showed 'Foundling' at the Royal Horticultural Society in London on 18 April 1972 and gained for it an Award of Merit. Since that show, it has continued to win prizes and has possibly won more than any other daffodil.

44 Cultivated by Michael Ward, Killiney, County Dublin, 30 April 1986. [×0.7]

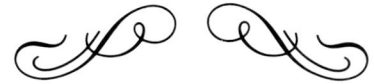

PLATE 45

Pelargonium 'Koko'

PLATE 45
Pelargonium 'Koko'

Geraniaceae

Pelargonium is the correct Latin name for the genus of perennial herbs from southern Africa which have yielded the popular "in-door geranium". In the wild, at least two hundred and fifty species of *Pelargonium* have been described, including a few species in Asia and Australasia. In southern Africa, they have diversified into many strange forms; some are succulent and almost cactus-like, some have woody, bulbous rootstocks.

African species were first introduced into European gardens during the second quarter of the seventeenth century after the Dutch colony was established at the Cape of Good Hope. By the beginning of the eighteenth century, they were known to gardeners in Ireland. Three different species were cultivated in the second Physic Garden established on the campus of the University of Dublin (see Introduction, p. 11), according to Professor William Stephens' manuscript catalogue of 1726; from the names cited, it is known that *P. capitatum* (L.) L'Hérit. and *P. alchemilloides* (L.) L'Hérit. were among the small collection. As botanical exploration of the Cape region progressed during the seventeenth and eighteenth centuries, more and more species were introduced into Europe, and as greenhouses were being continually improved, congenial conditions were soon readily available for the cultivation of these species.

The ivy-leaved race of *Pelargonium* cultivars was developed from *P. peltatum* (L.) L'Hérit., a species native in the Eastern Cape. It reached Europe in 1700, introduced by Willem Adriaan van der Stel, and probably came to Britain in 1774. Over many decades this species has yielded, through deliberate selection and breeding, numerous named cultivars ranging in colour from white to deep purple.

About 1972, an American tourist noticed a peculiar ivy-leaved *Pelargonium* growing in a small Mexican village – the plant had scarlet-pink petals with white centres. She obtained some cuttings and brought them to Mr Durren, a Californian nurseryman. He propagated it and gave some cuttings, in turn, to another nurseryman, William E. Schmidt. Henry Weller, a prominent member of the British and European Geranium Society, brought cuttings of this Mexican plant to Europe in 1973 and it was circulated in Europe. In the United States, the plant had been called 'Rouletta', but when Herr Topperwein, a Bavarian nurseryman, sought to register the cultivar name, he found that 'Roulette' was already in use, and he renamed the plant 'Mexikanerin' (subsequently, this was corrupted into 'Mexicana').

In 1977, Dr Alan Cassells, a native of Dublin, then at Wye College, obtained cuttings of 'Mexikanerin' and exhibited plants at the Chelsea Flower Show that year. Together with a postgraduate student George Minas, Dr Cassells set about investigating the cause of the so-called picotee effect – the dark margins around the pale centre to each petal. Their research revealed the presence of a virus, now called Pelargonium Petal Streak Agent (PPSA), infecting an old cultivar which proved to be 'Mexican Beauty'. The picotee effect is not always as marked as it is in 'Mexikanerin'; Dr Cassells and his colleagues discovered that it was influenced by such environmental factors as temperature at bud formation.

We usually think of viruses as harmful, causing the death of plants or unpleasant human afflications such as the common cold and influenza. But some viruses are relatively harmless; PPSA does not appear to have any adverse effect on the plants, but from the horticultural point of view, the infection is beneficial, yielding an attractive cultivar. The picotee-flowered series of ivy-leaved *Pelargonium* cultivars has become popular, and millions of plants are sold every year in Europe, Australasia and North America.

The discovery that the virus (PPSA) could be graft-transmitted made it possible to create new picotee-flowered cultivars of the ivy-leaved *Pelargonium* simply by grafting 'Mexikanerin' on to plants of existing cultivars; the new plants are termed 'transformed varieties', but the precise status of these transformed variants in terms of cultivar nomenclature is most uncertain at the present time. At Wye College, Dr Cassells raised a number of new picotee-flowered, ivy-leaved

continued on page 196

45 Cultivated by Mrs J. Cassells, Guileen, Whitegate, County Cork, 9 August 1985. [×0.7]

continued

cultivars, and some of the best of these were released under the series name Harlequin.

In 1979, Alan Cassells was appointed to the Chair of Botany in University College, Cork, where he has continued his work with ivy-leaved cultivars and the picotee effect, producing another new series of plants. His recent research has been centred on the production of more stable picotee-flowered cultivars, and the darkest of those so far produced is 'Koko'.

Pelargonium 'Koko' has glossy green leaves typical of the ivy-leaved cultivars. The flowers are "double" with about ten petals – the wild species of *Pelargonium* and all the single-flowered cultivars have only five petals. The individual petals have deep-purple margins and a white central streak; as mentioned, the degree of streaking varies and the petals may have a pale-lavender centre.

This cultivar was first synthesized by Judy Cassells in the spring of 1984 by transforming the cultivar 'Rio Grande' with Pelargonium Petal Streak Agent. It will be released in 1987 by Plant Biotechnology UCC Ltd, a company set up in 1983 by University College, Cork, to commercialize some of the research carried out in the Department of Plant Science (formerly the Department of Botany).

'Koko' is a Japanese term signifying the proper respect of the son for his father.

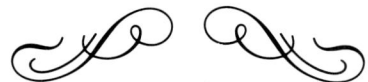

PLATE 46

Brownea × crawfordii Watson

PLATE 46
Brownea × *crawfordii* Watson

Papilionaceae

Brownea is a genus of evergreen, leguminous trees found only in tropical South and Central America and in the West Indies. There are perhaps six different species, but the taxonomy of the genus is notoriously difficult and as many as twelve species have been listed in garden catalogues. The genus was named in honour of Dr Patrick Browne (*c*. 1720–1790), a native of County Mayo and the author of *Civil and Natural History of Jamaica*, which was published in 1756. Browne's family had property in the West Indies and he spent many years living in Antigua, Jamaica and St Croix before finally returning to his native county and settling at Rushbrook near Ballinrobe. He compiled a manuscript flora of western Ireland, but died in 1790 before it could be published.

As *Brownea* is native in tropical forests, it cannot be cultivated out-of-doors in Ireland or Britain; it must be kept in a heated glasshouse where the minimum winter temperature is about 20°C. There is a single plant of *Brownea* (possibly *B. coccinea* Jacq.) in the National Botanic Gardens, Dublin, and as far as is known, it is the only plant of the genus in cultivation in Ireland. Last century, however, William H. Crawford of Lakelands, Cork, grew many of the species. It is recorded that in 1873 Crawford had a collection of twelve species, but Dr M. T. Masters succinctly commented that many of the names applied to Crawford's plants were 'probably botanical names for hybrids – names, at any rate, of which we find no record in botanical works, or in the Kew herbarium.' At least three hybrids were raised in his garden and plants of these hybrids were bequeathed to the Glasnevin Botanic Gardens and the Royal Botanic Gardens, Kew. One was named *B*. × *crawfordii* in memory of its originator.

Brownea × *crawfordii* was raised when plants labelled *B. grandiceps* Jacq. and *B. macrophylla* M. T. Masters were cross-pollinated. A single plant was sent to Kew after Crawford's death in 1888; it flowered there in 1891 and is still in cultivation – our plate was prepared from flowers received from Kew in 1984. Another plant came to Glasnevin about the same time and flowered in 1890; it is no longer living. Among the other hybrids were seedlings of *B. coccinea* × *B. latifolia* Jacq., for which William Gumbleton, a friend of Crawford and a fellow Cork gardener, suggested the name *B*. × *lakelandsensis*.

The leaves of *Brownea* species and hybrids are pinnate, up to 75 cm long, with from six to ten pairs of leaflets; each leaflet is elliptical, about 5 cm wide and up to 20 cm long. When young, they hang limply from the branches and are tinged red, but as they mature they become dark green and somewhat leathery. The flowers are borne in trusses up to 20 cm in diameter which, from a distance, resemble the flower-clusters of some of the larger rhododendrons. Each inflorescence contains about fifty individual blossoms, which are bright red in colour and about 10 cm long. The flower is composed of a whorl of five petals, ten stamens and a single central ovary surmounted by a curved style. The stamens exceed the petals, which are 4 cm long.

William Crawford's garden at Lakelands no longer exists. However, he is not forgotten in Cork, for he endowed the Crawford Municipal College of Art. Crawford also provided funds for a fine range of glasshouses that was erected for the Department of Botany at University College, Cork. And as well as this fine hybrid, Crawford's garden is remembered as the first place where *Magnolia campbellii* Hook. f. & Thoms. flowered in the British Isles.

46 Cultivated in Royal Botanic Gardens, Kew, Surrey, 8 March 1984. [×0.6]

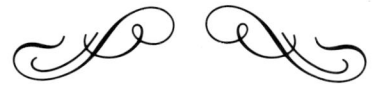

PLATE 47
Prunus subhirtella Miquel
'Autumnalis'

PLATE 47
Prunus subhirtella Miquel
'Autumnalis'

Rosaceae

October cherry, Jagatsu-zakura

Prunus contains about two hundred species, including the blackthorn (*P. spinosa* L.), bird-cherry (*P. padus* L.) and wild cherry or gean (*P. avium* (L.) L.) which are native in Ireland. Also included is the cherry laurel (*P. laurocerasus* L.) which is frequently naturalized in large gardens and estates. Important edible fruits and nuts, including almond, peach, apricot and plum, are produced from cultivated species of *Prunus*, and equally significant are the numerous species and cultivars which are grown simply for their beautiful flowers. For many centuries, flowering cherries have been planted in gardens, especially in Japan whence came some of the finest cultivars. The now ubiquitous double-pink cherry called 'Kanzan' is perhaps the best-known Japanese cultivar. There are many others, but they are not as common in Irish gardens.

Prunus subhirtella is a Japanese species. It is widely cultivated in Japan, where innumerable cultivars have been selected and propagated. 'Autumnalis' is one of the old Japanese cultivars and it first reached Ireland in the spring of 1901. It was introduced by Daisy Hill Nursery, Newry, County Down, under the name "*P. miqueliana*". Thomas Smith, the nursery's founder, distributed a few plants soon after its arrival. In December 1913, the cherry flowered in the Royal Botanic Gardens, Kew, and specimens were sent to Professor Koehne in Berlin; he identified it as a variety of a species that he had described and named the previous year, *P. microlepis* Koehne, and suggested that this cherry should be named *P. microlepis* var. *smithii* Koehne. But that name was soon abandoned when the cherry was identified as a cultivar of *P. subhirtella*. It appeared under that specific name in the Daisy Hill Nursery's catalogue (no. 101), which was published about 1923; it was still a rare plant at that time and the price of a young tree was not printed in the catalogue, being available only 'on application'.

The Japanese name for this cherry may be translated as October cherry, and this encapsulates the cultivar's most noteworthy characteristic; it flowers twice, once in the autumn or early winter, and again in the following spring. In Ireland, this means that *P. subhirtella* 'Autumnalis' is in bloom in November and again in April and May.

Prunus subhirtella 'Autumnalis' forms a small tree, perhaps reaching 7 or 8 m in height, with a spreading canopy of thin, twiggy branches. The bark is very dark grey. The autumn flush of blossom appears after the leaves have fallen; these flowers have short pedicels, little more than 0.5 cm long. In the spring, the flowers have much longer (*c.* 3 cm) pedicels and they open before the young foliage has emerged. The individual flowers are fragrant, blush-pink fading almost to white if the weather is sunny, and they hang in clusters from the bare branches. 'Autumnalis' is a "double-flowered" cherry; there are ten to fifteen petals in each blossom instead of the normal five. According to W. J. Bean, this cultivar never sets fruits, and I have certainly not observed any on trees in Ireland. When out of flower, *P. subhirtella*, like so many of its relatives, is not in any way distinguished; the foliage is dull green and the habit is unremarkable.

The October cherry has to be propagated by grafting on to *Prunus* stock or by rooting cuttings. It is tolerant of lime-rich soil, but is best sited against a background of dark-foliaged evergreens, so that the small, pale-pink flowers can be seen to good effect.

Lady Moore (see Plate 34) wrote that Thomas Smith 'deserves the gratitude of all plant-lovers for having been the first to draw attention to the merits' of this flowering cherry. While not raised in Ireland, the connections between this Japanese cultivar and the Daisy Hill Nursery, which celebrates its centenary in 1987, warrant its inclusion in this *Florilegium*.

47 Cultivated by Mrs W. Fennell, Burtown, Athy, County Kildare, 27 December 1985, and (uppermost stem only) Trinity College, Dublin, 17 January 1986. [×0.7]

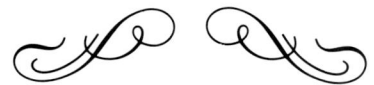

PLATE 48

Rosa 'Irish Elegance'

PLATE 48
Rosa 'Irish Elegance'

Rosaceae

Ireland has been renowned for the breeding of two groups of garden plants: daffodils and roses. Daffodils such as 'Cantatrice' (AIF I: Plate 37), 'Kingscourt' (AIF I: Plate 38) and 'Foundling' (Plate 44) represent the achievements of Irish daffodil enthusiasts over the last century. As for roses, chance sports, for example, 'Souvenir de St Anne's' (AIF I: Plate 25), do not typify the deliberate work of Irish rose breeders; they are a very minor aspect of Ireland's contribution to the development of fine roses, having no direct connection with the craft of creating new cultivars.

Modern roses, it must be confessed, are not the special favourites of either the artist or the author of this work. That is not to say that we denigrate modern cultivars – it is merely a matter of our personal tastes.

The pressures of rose trials and horticultural competitions, as well as the constraints of commercial production, combine today to compel rose breeders to produce roses that are easy to market and sell in hundreds of thousands, roses that are prim and perfect, or overblown and blowzy. These are not unworthy attributes, but somehow the modern rose has become rather synthetic in manner and has lost charm and some of the simple appeal of this ancient garden flower. A few breeders have now diverged from the mainstream and begun breeding roses which are more akin to the 'old-fashioned' cultivars of earlier centuries; they are attempting to raise cultivars that have grace, vigour and character. But, as in so many arts, personal opinions and prejudices divide us into admirers and critics.

The principal rose breeder in Ireland today is Patrick Dickson, whose family has been breeding roses for more than a century at Newtownards in County Down. Until 1972, McGredy's Nursery at Portadown in County Armagh was Dickson's keen rival. In that year, Sam McGredy moved his business to New Zealand, ending that family's nine decades in Ireland. There were other breeders – Hugh Dickson of Belfast, for example – and there are several people, including Sean McCann and Pat Slattery, who have raised and introduced roses in recent years, but none can compete in numbers or in quality with the two Northern Ireland nurseries.

McGredy's roses are still widely cultivated; such cultivars as 'Piccadilly', 'Rose of Tralee', 'Mrs Sam McGredy', 'Handel' and 'Picasso' remain in catalogues. Of Dickson's cultivars, among the more familiar are perhaps 'Dickson's Flame', 'Grandpa Dickson', 'Red Devil' and 'Peek-a-boo'. Patrick Dickson continues to produce superb plants, but does not market them himself, and in 1986 his rose 'Gentle Touch' won the prestigious (and coveted) title Rose of the Year.

More than one thousand different roses have been bred, named and introduced by Irish nurseries since 1887, most of them by Dicksons of Hawlmark and McGredy of Portadown. To choose one rose from among those for inclusion in this *Florilegium* was not an easy task, but in the end we selected one of the Dicksons' old cultivars, 'Irish Elegance'. The main reason for its choice is the simplicity and elegance of the blossom – very few modern cultivars have single flowers, five-petalled. We hope it is a fitting tribute to one of Ireland's greatest nurseries, now over one and a half centuries old.

Stimulated by the success of a Wiltshire man, Henry Bennett, in showing some "Pedigree Hybrids" in 1878, George Dickson of Newtownards began the following year trying to breed better roses. His two sons Alexander and George assisted, and after the early, not-unexpected, failures they did succeed in producing three new cultivars, which were shown in London in 1886; 'Earl of Dufferin', 'Lady Helen Stewart' and 'Miss Ethel Brownlow' were the roses. In 1887, this "First set of Pedigree Seedlings" was offered for sale by Dicksons. For the remaining years of the century, the business of breeding roses developed steadily, and by the beginning of the 1900s, Dicksons of Hawlmark were established as a leading international nursery. They raised as many as three thousand seedling roses each year and had begun winning some of their many gold medals. The Dicksons attempted to produce a race of hardy, free-flowering plants; in particular, the firm raised a series of single-

continued on page 208

48 Cultivated by Mrs S. Walker, Fernhill, Sandyford, County Dublin, 29 June 1986. [×0.8]

continued

flowered hybrid-tea roses which were vigorous and flowered for most of the summer. These bore names prefixed by "Irish" – the series included 'Irish Beauty' (1900), 'Irish Brightness' (1903), 'Irish Engineer' (1904), 'Irish Glory' (1900), 'Irish Harmony' (1904), 'Irish Modesty' (1900), 'Irish Pride' (1903) and 'Irish Star' (1903). These were described in their catalogues and eulogized by W. J. Grant in *Flora and Sylva*.

'Irish Elegance' was another, recently described by Jack Harkness as 'that evidence of good taste in Newtownards'. Introduced in 1905, the catalogue entry may be quoted, for it well describes this rose: 'This we consider the most charming variety of all the single roses we have raised. It is a gem of the first water. In the bud state it is bronzy orange scarlet, which whilst expanding assumes varied apricot hues which, in contrast, lend to it a charm peculiarly its own. It is of vigorous and erect growth, branching freely, and is a profuse bloomer from early June until the extreme end of the flowering season. The spiral buds, expanding and expanded blossoms are of such exquisite distincture as to always draw attention, even in the midst of our seedling quarters, so that for button-holes or decoration it has distinct features all its own. When known we predict this unique rose will create quite a furore.' The prediction did not, perhaps, come fully to fruition, but 'Irish Elegance' gained a Wisley Rose Award (class II) after trials by the Royal Horticultural Society in England.

As well as the single hybrid-tea roses, the Dicksons initiated their own lineage of double-flowered roses. 'Killarney', introduced in 1898, was silvery-pink, as was the much later 'Silver Lining' of 1959, but those are merely random names plucked from a litany of fine plants. Most recently, Patrick Dickson has developed his own unique series of "patio" roses, diminutive plants, free-flowering and eminently suited to the modern suburban garden; 'Gentle Touch' is one of that new race. It also has the charm of the older single hybrid-tea roses, for the tight, urn-shaped buds open fully to a saucer of pale pink filled with yellow stamens.

But what of the old cultivars, the century of breeding, the 'science of pure experiment'? Fortunately, many survive and are still cherished. At Mount Stewart, near Newtownards, 'Dame Edith Helen', described as a 'huge pink rose with glorious fragrance', has been restored in recent years to beds beside the house in which Dame Edith Helen, as the Marchioness of Londonderry, lived and around which she created a superb garden. 'Ards Rover', a fine, red-flowered, climbing rose, is still in cultivation. The others that are extant should be preserved, for they record the progress of gardening in Ireland and the changing tastes of gardeners, as well as the progression in the craft of plant breeding. Although they are old-fashioned and perhaps not as vigorous nor as disease-resistant as newer cultivars, they testify to the skill of dedicated plantsmen.

One of the pleasures we have gained while preparing the two volumes that now compose *An Irish Florilegium* has been the thrill of discovering that many of the cultivars raised in Ireland in olden days still flourish in our gardens. If plants such as *Rosa* 'Irish Elegance' vanish, if *R.* × *hibernica* does become extinct in gardens as well as in its native habitat, we will all be losers.

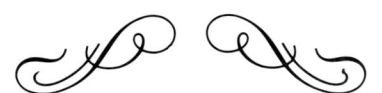

LIST OF PLATES
BIBLIOGRAPHY
INDEX

LIST OF PLATES

1. *Rosa × hibernica*
2. *Carex buxbaumii*
3. *Lathyrus japonicus* ssp. *maritimus*
4. *Adiantum capillus-veneris*
5. *Saxifraga hirsuta*
   Saxifraga spathularis
   Saxifraga × polita
6. *Hieracium scullyi*
7. *Campanula rotundifolia*
8. *Oxalis acetosella*
9. *Allium babingtonii*
10. *Scilla verna*
11. *Erica erigena*
    Erica erigena f. *alba*
12. *Fuchsia magellanica*
13. *Sisyrinchium angustifolium*
14. *Trollius europaeus*
15. *Anemone nemorosa* 'Lady Doneraile'
    Anemone nemorosa 'Lucy's Wood'
16. *Primula vulgaris*
    Primula vulgaris 'Elizabeth Dickey'
17. *Primula edgeworthii*
18. *Buddleja crispa*
19. *Lonicera tragophylla*
20. *Oxypetalum coeruleum*
21. *Dionaea muscipula*
22. *Olearia* 'Henry Travers'
23. *Crinum moorei*
24. *Littonia modesta*
25. *Mackaya bella*
26. *Abutilon vitifolium*
27. *Rosa bracteata*
28. *Rubus lasiostylus*
29. *Helleborus lividus*
30. *Anemone coronaria* 'Saint Brigid'
31. *Azara microphylla* 'Variegata'
32. *Rhododendron* 'Mulroy Vanguard'
33. *Rhododendron* 'Evelyn Slinger'
34. *Cytisus* 'Lady Moore'
    Cytisus 'Killiney Red'
35. *Hebe* 'Headfortii'
36. *Nerine* 'Glensavage Gem'
    Nerine 'John Fanning'
37. *Anthemis* 'Grallagh Gold'
38. *Sambucus nigra* f. *porphyrophylla* 'Guincho Purple'
39. *Bergenia* 'Ballawley'
40. *Primula* 'Rowallane Rose'
41. *Hypericum* 'Rowallane'
42. *Ilex × altaclerensis* 'Hendersonii'
    Ilex × altaclerensis 'Lawsoniana'
43. *Papaver* 'Fireball'
44. *Narcissus* 'Foundling'
45. *Pelargonium* 'Koko'
46. *Brownea × crawfordii*
47. *Prunus subhirtella* 'Autumnalis'
48. *Rosa* 'Irish Elegance'

LIST OF PLATES
in the first volume of *An Irish Florilegium*

1. *Sorbus hibernica*
2. *Dryas octopetala*
3. *Potentilla fruticosa*
4. *Gentiana verna*
5. *Trichomanes speciosum*
6. *Geranium sanguineum*
7. *Iris pseudoacorus*
8. *Simethis planifolia*
9. *Euphorbia hyberna*
10. *Pinguicula grandiflora*
11. *Sarracenia purpurea*
12. *Otanthus maritimus*
13. *Primula veris*
14. *Arbutus unedo*
15. *Erica mackaiana*
16. *Erica ciliaris*
17. *Daboecia cantabrica*
    Daboecia cantabrica f. *alba*
    Daboecia cantabrica 'Praegerae'
18. *Ulex europaeus*
    Ulex europaeus 'Strictus'
19. *Taxus baccata* 'Lutea'
    Taxus baccata 'Fastigiata'
20. *Primula* × *pubescens* 'Old Irish Blue'
21. *Myrtus apiculata* 'Glanleam Gold'
22. *Eucryphia* × *nymansensis* 'Mount Usher'
23. *Paeonia* 'Anne Rosse'
24. *Garrya* × *issaquahensis*
    Garrya × *issaquahensis* 'Pat Ballard'
25. *Rosa* 'Souvenir de Saint Anne's'
26. *Potentilla* 'Sophie's Blush'
27. *Chaenomeles* × *superba* 'Rowallane'
28. *Forsythia* × *intermedia* 'Lynwood'
29. *Meconopsis* × *sheldonii* 'Slieve Donard'
30. *Pittosporum tenuifolium* 'Silver Queen'
31. *Mahonia* × *media* 'Charity'
32. *Escallonia rubra* 'C. F. Ball'
33. *Solanum crispum* 'Glasnevin'
34. *Rhododendron arboreum* 'Fernhill'
35. *Calceolaria* × *burbidgei*
36. *Galanthus* 'Straffan'
    Galanthus 'Hill Poë'
37. *Narcissus* 'Cantatrice'
38. *Narcissus* 'Kingscourt'
39. *Penstemon fruticosus* var. *scouleri* 'Alba'
40. *Romneya coulteri*
41. *Abelia triflora*
42. *Viburnum utile*
43. *Lilium henryi*
44. *Hamamelis mollis*
45. *Davidia involucrata*
46. *Rhododendron augustinii*
47. *Rhododendron burmanicum*
48. *Coelogyne mooreana*

BIBLIOGRAPHY

INTRODUCTION

The Introduction is based on published and unpublished sources. The latter include manuscripts in the archives of the University of Dublin, the National Botanic Gardens, Glasnevin, and the Royal Botanic Gardens, Kew; fuller information on these is given in the detailed bibliographies to Nelson (1982, 1987), and Nelson and McCracken (1987) – see below.

Anonymous. 1983. *Gids voor de Hortus Botanicus der Rijksuniversiteit te Leiden*. (Leiden)

Anonymous. [1986]. *Report [of] the Dublin : Cambridge Expedition to Mauritius for plant conservation 1985*. [Dublin]

A. Crookshank. 1986. The Long Room. *Treasures of the Library, Trinity College, Dublin* (edited by P. Fox): pp 16–28. (Dublin)

E. Hill. 1803. *An address to the students in physic*. (Dublin)

E. Hill. 1805. *An address to the President and Fellows of the... College of Physicians in Ireland*. (Dublin)

P. W. Jackson. [1986]. *The story of the Botanic Gardens of Trinity College, Dublin 1687–1787*. (Dublin)

P. W. Jackson, Q. Cronk and J. Parnell. 1986. Mauritian palm – saved? *Threatened Plants Newsletter 16*: 12–13.

E. M. McCracken. 1979. The Botanic Garden, Trinity College, Dublin. *Garden History 7 (1)*: 86–90.

R. B. McDowell and D. A. Webb. 1982. *Trinity College, Dublin, 1592–1952: an academic history*. (Cambridge)

E. C. Nelson. 1978. *Todea barbara* in the National Botanic Gardens, Dublin. *The Garden 103*: 418.

E. C. Nelson. 1982. The influence of Leiden on botany in Dublin in the early eighteenth century. *Huntia 4*: 133–146.

E. C. Nelson. 1984. *An Irish Flower Garden*. (Kilkenny)

E. C. Nelson. 1987. 'In honour of Ireland' – the Hibernian contribution to *Curtis's Botanical Magazine* 1787–1987. *Kew Magazine 4*: 39–51.

E. C. Nelson (in press). The Scottish influence on botany and horticulture in Ireland. *Scottish Naturalist*.

E. C. Nelson and E. M. McCracken. 1987. *The Brightest Jewel: a history of the National Botanic Gardens, Glasnevin, Dublin*. (Kilkenny)

F. A. Stafleu. 1969. Botanical gardens before 1818. *Boissiera 14*: 31–46.

W. T. Stearn. 1962. The influence of Leyden on botany in the seventeenth and eighteenth centuries. *British Journal for the History of Science 1*: 137–158.

J. W. Stubbs. 1889. *The history of the University of Dublin...* (Dublin)

NOTES ON THE PLATES

The sources consulted are listed according to the Plate number. Works listed above are quoted in the following bibliography simply by author and date (e.g., E. C. Nelson. 1984).

1. J. Templeton. 1803. A letter... on a new species of rose. *Transactions of the Dublin Society 3*: 162–164. R. Melville. 1975. *Rosa*; in C. A. Stace. *Hybridization and the flora of the British Isles*: pp 212–227. (London). E. C. Nelson. 1984: pp 25–28. W. Williams. 1959. *Report of the John Innes Institute 49*: 7–13.

2. T. Colby. 1837. *Ordnance Survey of the County of Londonderry. Memoir of the... parish of Templemore*. Appendix: pp 6–13. (Dublin: 2nd edition). A. C. Jermy, A. O. Chater and R. W. David. 1982. *Sedges of the British Isles:* pp 192–193. (London: 2nd edition). R. L. Praeger. 1938. *A flora of the north-east of Ireland*: pp 241–242. (Belfast: 2nd edition)

3. E. C. Nelson (in press). Exotic drift fruits and seeds on British coasts. *Proceedings of the Royal Institution of Cornwall* (in press). Stella M. Turk (personal communication). The assistance of Laurie Williams (Hayle) and of Roger and Des Lidstone (Penryn) is also gratefully acknowledged.

4. J. Gerard. 1597. *Herball*. (London). D. M. Synnott. n.d. *Irish ferns*. (Dublin: Irish Environmental Library Series, no. 68)

5. R. W. Scully. 1910. *Flora of County Kerry*: pp 95–106. (Dublin). D. A. Webb. 1950. Hybridization and variation in the Robertsonian saxifrages. *Proceedings of the Royal Irish Academy 53 (B 9)*: 85–97.

6. W. R. Linton. 1905. *An account of the British Hieracia*. (London)

7. A. G. More. 1876. Report on the flora of Inishbofin, Galway. *Proceedings of the Royal Irish Academy 2*: 553–578.

8. J. R. Packham. 1978. *Oxalis acetosella* L. *Journal of Ecology 66*: 669–693.

9. E. C. Nelson. 1984: pp 94–95. W. T. Stearn. 1978. European species of *Allium* and allied genera of Alliaceae: a synonymic enumeration. *Annales Musei Goulandris 4*: 83–198.

10. J. Templeton MSS. (Ulster Museum, Belfast)

11. P. J. Foss, G. J. Doyle and E. C. Nelson. 1987. The distribution of *Erica erigena*. R. Ross in Ireland. *Watsonia 16*: 311–327. B. D. Morley. 1974. *Erica erigena*: the origin of the specific epithet. *Journal of the Royal Horticultural Society 99*: 463. D. A. Webb. 1984. The flora of Ireland in its European context. *Journal of Life Sciences, Royal Dublin Society 4*: 143–160.

12. E. C. Nelson (unpublished data). D. M. Synnott. 1979. Folklore, legend and Irish plants. *Irish gardening and horticulture* (edited by E. C.

Nelson and A. Brady): pp 36–43. (Dublin). J. Templeton. 1802. On the naturalization of plants. *Transactions of the Royal Irish Academy 8*: 111–129 [read 1799].

13. M. Guedes. 1969. Typification of *Sisyrinchium bermudianum* and *S. angustifolium* (Iridaceae). *Taxon 18*: 542–545. L. M. Hill. 1983. Chromosomal typification of *Sisyrinchium bermudianum* L. (Iridaceae). *Rhodora 85*: 257–258. A. D. Löve and D. Löve. 1961. Some nomenclatural changes in the European flora 1: Species and supra-specific categories. *Botaniska Notiser 114*: 37–38.

14. N. Colgan and R. W. Scully. 1898. *Cybele Hibernica*: p 11. (Dublin: 2nd edition)

15. W. Robinson. 1900. The large blue wood anemone. *The Garden 57*: 3. E. A. Bowles. 1914. *My garden in spring*: pp 209–215. (London). E. C. Nelson. 1984: pp 137–138. U. Toubol. 1981. Clonal variation in *Anemone nemorosa*. *The Plantsman 3*: 167–174.

16. E. C. Nelson. 1984. Primroses. *Irish Garden Plant Society Newsletter 12* (Supplement) [reprinted in *National Primrose and Auricula Society (Southern) Yearbook*: 56–63]; *Irish Garden Plant Society Newsletter 14* (Supplement). Dr Molly Sanderson (personal communication)

17. W. W. Smith and H. R. Fletcher. 1944. The genus *Primula*: section Petiolares. *Transactions of the Royal Society of Edinburgh 61*: 290–291.

18. C. Colvin and E. C. Nelson (in press). 'Building castles of flowers': Maria Edgeworth as gardener. *Garden History* (in press). J. Ewan. 1980. The transit of botany from Ireland to America. *Glasra 4*: 1–11. E. C. Nelson. 1984: pp 65–67.

19. S. A. Skan. 1906. *Lonicera tragophylla*. *Botanical Magazine*, tab. 8064. E. C. Nelson. 1984: pp 168–169.

20. W. J. Hooker. 1838. *Tweedia versicolor*. *Botanical Magazine*, tab. 3630. D. Don. 1837. *Tweedia coerulea*. *Botanical Register*, tab. 407. E. C. Nelson. 1984: p 182. J. Tweedie MSS. (Royal Botanic Gardens, Kew)

21. W. Bartram. 1791. *Travels through North and South Carolina*... (Salt Lake City: reprinted edition of 1980, introduced by R. M. Peck). W. Darlington. 1849. *Memorials of John Bartram and Humphrey Marshall*. (New York: facsimile edition of 1967, edited by J. Ewan). J. Ewan. 1968. *William Bartram, botanical and zoological drawings, 1756–1788*. (Philadelphia). L. W. Dillwyn. 1843. *Hortus Collinsonianus*: pp 18–19 (Swansea). S. Savage. 1948. *Catalogue of the manuscripts in the library of the Linnean Society of London: IV Calendar of the Ellis manuscripts*. (London)

22. E. C. Nelson. 1984: pp 78–79. E. C. Nelson and E. M. McCracken. 1987: pp 166–168.

23. J. D. Hooker. 1874. *Crinum moorei*. *Botanical Magazine*, tab. 6113.

24. W. J. Hooker. 1853. *Littonia modesta*. *Botanical Magazine*, tab. 4723. E. C. Nelson and E. M. McCracken. 1987: pp 78–96.

25. W. H. Harvey. 1859. On a new genus and two new species of plants from the Cape of Good Hope. *Proceedings of the Dublin University Zoological and Botanical Association 1*: 253–254.

26. E. C. Nelson. 1984: pp 92–93.

27. E. Bretschneider. 1898. *History of European botanical discoveries in China*. Vol. 1: pp 156–183. (London)

28. J. D. Hooker. 1895. *Rubus lasiostylus*. *Botanical Magazine*, tab. 7426. E. C. Nelson. 1984. The garden history of Augustine Henry's plants. *The wood and the trees, a biography of Augustine Henry*, by Sheila Pim: pp 217–236. (Kilkenny: 2nd edition)

29. J. D. Hooker. 1903. *Helleborus lividus*. *Botanical Magazine*, tab. 7903. E. C. Nelson. 1984: pp 82–83. Additional information from Dr I. K. Ferguson (personal communication) and manuscripts in the National Botanic Gardens, Glasnevin, and Trinity College Botanic Garden, Dublin.

30. Information on Geashill anemones was made available by Dr J. G. D. Lamb (personal communication). F. W. Burbidge. 1900. Mrs Alice Louisa Lawrenson. *The Garden 57*: 230. E. C. Nelson. 1984: pp 150–151.

31. S. Arnott. 1908. Belgrove, County Cork. *Gardeners' Chronicle 44 (ser. 3)*: 424.

32. M. Forrest. 1986. *Rhododendron* 'Mulroy Vanguard', a newly-registered cultivar. *Moorea 5*: 17.

33. My thanks to Archie Bingham and Jack Murray for their assistance.

34. Information from catalogues published by Watson of Killiney, and from Hugh Watson, Glengarriff.

35. E. C. Nelson. 1984: pp 127–128.

36. My thanks to Miss Sheila Findlater for her assistance, and to Tony Norris.

37. E. C. Nelson. 1984: p 160.

38. E. C. Nelson. 1986. Purple-leaved elders. *The Plantsman 8*: 189–190.

39. P. F. Yeo. 1971. Cultivation of *Bergenia* (Saxifragaceae) in the British Isles. *Baileya 18*: 100–101. Additional information from David Shaw-Smith, and from published catalogues of Ballawley Nursery.

40. G. S. Thomas. 1950. Some famous Irish gardens. *Journal of the Royal Horticultural Society 75*: 237.

41. N. K. B. Robson. 1985. Studies in the genus *Hypericum* L. *Bulletin of the British Museum (Natural History) Botany 12 (4)*: 244–245.

42. S. Andrews. 1982. Hollies in Ireland. *Moorea 1*: 5–15. S. Andrews. 1983. Notes on some *Ilex × altaclerensis* clones. *The Plantsman 5*: 65–81. (The Hodginses are mentioned by J. T. Mackay. 1836. *Flora Hibernica*: pp 66, 84. Both J. Hodgins and R. Hodgins are stated by Mackay to be nurserymen.)

43. B. Mathew. 1985. *Papaver orientale* 'Nanum Flore Pleno'. *The Garden 110*: 271–274 (see also *The Garden 110*: 538).

44. My thanks to Mrs Reade for her assistance.

45. My thanks to Professor Alan Cassells, University College, Cork, for his assistance.

46. T. Crawford and E. C. Nelson. 1979. Irish horticulturists I: W. H. Crawford. *Garden History 7 (2)*: 23–26. W. E. Gumbleton. 1891. *Brownea × crawfordii*. *Gardeners' Chronicle 9 (ser. 3)*: 439. W. Watson. 1891. Kew notes. *The Garden 9 (ser. 3)*: 398.

47. E. C. Nelson. 1984: pp 38–39.

48. My thanks to Patrick Dickson for his help. W. G. Grant. 1903. Beautiful Irish roses. *Flora and Sylva 1*: 265–269. J. Harkness. 1985. *The makers of heavenly roses*: pp 43–57. (London)

INDEX

References to the first volume of *An Irish Florilegium* are preceded by the Roman numeral I; those to the present volume by II. Entries in **bold** type indicate plants depicted in the plates and their main descriptive texts.

(1) Botanical and horticultural names

Abelia I: 154
  triflora I: 20, 28, **194–195**; II: 86
Abutilon vitifolium II: **118–119**
Acacia II: 138
Aconitum II: 74
Adiantum capillus-veneris I: 10; II: **30–31**, 58
Akebia quinata II: 122
Allium ampeloprasum II: 50
  babingtonii II: 8, **50–51**
  halleri II: 50
Allmania II: 116
Aloe II: 11
Ammophila arenaria I: 78
Amorphophallus kerrii II: 13
Androsace lanuginosa II: 13
Anemone II: 74
  coronaria II: 134–136
    'De Caen' II: 134
    'Saint Brigid' II: **134–136**
  'Lady Ardilaun' I: 130
  nemorosa II: 74–76
    'Currie's Pink' II: 74
    'Green Dream' II: 76
    'Green Fingers' II: 76
    'Hannah Gubbay' II: 76
    'Lady Doneraile' II: **74–75**
    'Lismore Blue' II: 74
    'Lismore Pink' II: 74
    'Lucy's Wood' II: **74–75**
    'Robinsoniana' II: 74
    'Robinsoniana Cornubiense' II: 76
  obtusiloba f. *patula* I: 218
Anthemis 'Beauty of Grallagh' II: 162
  'Grallagh Glory' II: 162
  'Grallagh Gold' II: **162–163**
  sancti-johannis II: 162
  tinctoria II: 162
Aquilegia II: 74
  vulgaris II: 74
Arbutus unedo I: 8–10, 62, **86–88**; II: 14, 34, 58
  'Croomei' I: 88
  f. *rubra* I: 88
Arctotis gumbeltonii I: 19
Arenaria ciliata I: 10
Asclepias II: 94
Asphodelus I: 62
Astragalus chinensis II: 122
Asystasia II: 114
Aubrieta II: 170
  'Amethyst' II: 170
  'Ballawley Giant' II: 170
  'Pink Parakeet' II: 170
Azara microphylla II: 138
    'Belgroviana' II: 138
    'Variegata' II: **138–139**

Begonia I: 24
Berberis I: 20, 154, 158
  × *antoniana* I: 22
  tsarongensis I: 20
Bergenia II: 170
  'Ballawley' II: **170–171**
  beesiana II: 170
  cordifolia II: 170
  delavayi II: 170
  'Delbees' II: 170
  'Distinction' II: 170
  'Profusion' II: 170
  purpurascens II: 170
  × *smithii* II: 170
Betula jacquemontii I: 27
Bossiaea II: 116
Brachyglottis repanda II: 13
Brownea coccinea II: 198
  × ***crawfordii*** II: **198–199**
  lakelandsensis II: 198
  latifolia II: 198
  macrophylla II: 198
Buddleja II: 86
  caryopteridifolia II: 86
  colvilei I: 19; II: 86
  crispa I: 28, 194; II: 84, **86–88**
  davidii II: 86, 88
    'Glasnevin Blue' II: 86
  farreri II: 86
  globosa II: 62, 86
Burbidgea II: 14, 116

Caesalpinia bonduc II: 26
Calamagrostis stricta II: 22
Calceolaria × *ballii* I: 158, 170
  × ***burbidgei*** I: 20–21, **170–171**
  fougetii I: 170
  integrifolia I: 170
  pavonii I: 170
  reflexa I: 170
Caltha palustris II: 74
Camellia I: 18
Campanula I: 20
  garganica 'W.H. Paine' II: 150
  rotundifolia II: **42–43**
    var. *speciosum* II: 42
  trachelium II: 42
Cardiocrinum giganteum I: 28, 194; II: 86
Carex buxbaumii II: 8, **22–23**
Cassiope fastigiata I: 194
Ceanothus I: 22
Cephalotus follicularis I: 13
Cercis racemosa I: 210
Chaenomeles japonica I: 138
  speciosa I: 138
  'Anemonefield Scarlet' I: 138
  'Phylis Moore' I: 138
  'Simonii' I: 138
  × ***superba* 'Rowallane'** I: 20, 22, **138–139**; II: 146, 178
Chamaecyparis lawsoniana II: 150
  'Kilbogget Gold' II: 150
  'Killiney' II: 150
  'Killiney Gold' II: 150
Circaea lutetiana II: 62
Clarkia II: 62
Clematis I: 38; II: 74
  montana I: 27
  vitalba I: 8, 38
Coelogyne mooreana I: **222–223**
Cordyline II: 15
Coreopsis drummondii I: 25
Cortaderia selloana I: 20; II: 94
Corynabutilon vitifolium II: 118
Coulteria II: 116
Crinum bulbispermum II: 106
  moorei II: 8, 15, **106–107**
  × *powellii* II: 106
Crocosmia masonorum I: 138; II: 178
Cydonia 'Rowallane Seedling' I: 138
Cytisus 'Andreanus' II: 150
  'C.E. Pearson' I: 22
  'Dorothy Walpole' I: 22
  'Firefly' I: 22; II: 150
  'Killiney Red' I: 22; II: **150–151**
  'Killiney Salmon' I: 22
  'Lady Moore' II: **150–151**
  scoparius II: 150

Daboecia azorica I: 98
  cantabrica I: 10, 12, 86, **98–99**; II: 34, 58
    f. *alba* I: 13, **98–99**
    'Bicolor' I: 98
    f. *blumii* II: 160
    'Charles Nelson' I: 98
    'Doris Findlater' II: 160
    'Porter's Variety' I: 98
    'Praegerae' I: **98–99**; II: 170
    'Tully' I: 98
Davidia involucrata I: 30, **210–212**
Delphinium II: 74
Deutzia × *elegantissima* I: 22
Dierama I: 22
  'Ariel' I: 22
  'Puck' I: 22
  'Titania' I: 22
Digitalis purpurea II: 114
Dionaea muscipula I: 25; II: **98–100**
Drosera anglica I: 8
Dryas octopetala I: 8, 10, **38–39**

Edgeworthia II: 84
Elaeocarpus II: 16
Embothrium coccineum 'Longifolium' I: 20
Entada gigas II: 26
Epilobium II: 62
Eremurus I: 62
Erica biformis I: 92
  carnea II: 60
    ssp. *occidentalis* II: 60
  ciliaris I: 62, 90, **94–95**
  cinerea I: 90
  crawfordii I: 90
  × *darleyensis* II: 60
  erigena I: 13, 90; II: **58–60**
    'Irish Dusk' II: **58–60**
    'Irish Salmon' II: 58
  herbacea II: 60
  hibernica II: 58
  mackaiana I: 13, **90–92**, 94; II: 34, 58, 114
    'Donegal' I: 90
    'Maura' I: 90
    'Plena' I: 90
    'William McCalla' I: 90
  × *praegeri* I: 90
  × *stuartii* I: 90
  tetralix I: 90, 94
  vagans I: 90
Eriocaulon I: 12
Eriophorum angustifolium II: 22
Erythropalum II: 114
Escallonia 'Alice' I: 158
  'Apple Blossom' I: 158
  'Glasnevin Hybrid' I: 158
  'Langleyensis' I: 158
  rosea I: 158
  'Rosette' I: 158
  ***rubra* 'C.F. Ball'** I: **158–159**
    var. *macrantha* I: 158
    var. *rubra* I: 158
  virgata I: 158
Eucalyptus I: 18
Eucryphia cordifolia I: 18, 118
  glutinosa I: 18, 118
    'Daisy Hill' I: 118
  × *intermedia* 'Rostrevor' I: 19, 118
  lucida I: 118
  × *nymansensis* I: 18, 118–119, 122
    'Nymansay' I: 118
    'Mount Usher' I: 18, **118–119**; II: 150
Eugenia apiculata I: 114
Euphorbia hyberna I: 62, **66–67**
  paralias I: 78
  pulcherrimum I: 66

***Forsythia* × *intermedia* 'Lynwood'** I: 15, 22, **142–143**; II: 146
  suspensa I: 42
  viridissima I: 142
Fuchsia coccinea II: 62
  gracilis II: 62
  magellanica II: 8, **62–64**
  'Riccartonii' II: 64

Galanthus II: 14
  caucasicus var. *grandis* I: 174
  'Hill Poë' I: 18, **174–176**; II: 162
  imperati I: 174
  nivalis I: 174
  plicatus I: 174
  'Straffan' I: 18, **174–176**
Garrya elliptica I: 126
  fremontii I: 126
  × ***issaquahensis*** I: **126–127**
    'Pat Ballard' I: 22, **126–127**
Gentiana verna I: 8, 10, **46–47**
Geranium sanguineum I: 8, 10, **54–55**
  traversii II: 62
Gloriosa superba II: 110
Godetia II: 62
Griselinia littoralis 'Bantry Bay' I: 19
Gunnera manicata II: 14

Hamamelis I: 154
  japonica I: 206
  mollis I: 31, **206–207**
  virginiana I: 206
Harveya II: 116
Hebe elliptica II: 154
  'Headfortii' I: 20; II: **154–155**
  macrocarpa II: 154
  traversii I: 27
Hedysarum latifolium II: 122
Helianthemum canum I: 13
Helleborus II: 14, 74
  argutifolius II: 130, 132
  corsicus II: 130
  lividus II: 13, 15, **130–132**
  niger II: 130
    'Saint Brigid' II: 134
  × *sternii* II: 130
Hieracium boreale II: 38
  hibernicum II: 38
  laevigatum II: 38
  scullyi II: **38–39**
  sparsifolium var. *oligodon* II: 38
  sparsifrons II: 38
Hoheria 'Glory of Amlwch' I: 22
Hyophorbe amaricaulis II: 16
Hypericum calycinum II: 178
  hookerianum I: 78
    'Rogersii' II: 178
  leschenaultii II: 178
  'Rowallane' I: 20, 22, 138; II: 146, **178–180**

Ilex × *altaclerensis* II: 182–184
    'Golden King' II: 184
    'Hendersonii' II: 8, **182–184**
    'Hendersonii Variegata' II: 184
    'Hodginsii' II: 182, 184
    'Lawsoniana' II: **182–184**
    'Shepherdii' II: 182
  aquifolium II: 182
    'Ferox' II: 182
  cornuta II: 122
  lawsonii II: 182
  perado II: 182, 184
  pernyi II: 182
Iris pseudoacorus I: 11, **58–59**
Itea ilicifolia I: 202

Kniphofia 'W.E. Gumbleton' I: 19
Kolkwitzia I: 194

Lathyrus japonicus* ssp. *maritimus II: **26–28**
Leptospermum 'Red Damask' I: 22
Leucojum I: 174
Ligustrum sinensis var. *stauntonii* II: 122
Lilium henryi I: 31, **202–203**; II: 90
  wallichianum I: 194
Littonia modesta II: 8, **110–111**
  var. *keitii* II: 110
Lobelia 'Firefly' I: 130
  'Lord Ardilaun' I: 130
  'Morning Glory' I: 130
Logania II: 86
Lonicera I: 194; II: 90
  henryi II: 90
  nitida II: 90, 138
  periclymenum II: 90
  pileata II: 90
  tragophylla II: **90–91**
Luma apiculata I: 114

Mackaia (Phaeophyceae) II: 164
Mackaya (Erythropalaceae) II: 164
Mackaya bella II: 8, 14, **114–116**
Macleaya cordata II: 122
Magnolia I: 18, 22, 154; II: 14
  campbellii II: 198
Mahonia I: 20, 154, 158
  lomariifolia I: 154
  × ***media* 'Charity'** I: **154–155**; II: 146
    'Charity's Sister' I: 154
    'Winter Sun' I: 154
Meconopsis × *beamishii* I: 146
  betonicifolia I: 146
  grandis I: 146
    'Prain's Variety' I: 146
    'Slieve Donard' I: 146
  × *sheldonii* I: 146–147
    'Ormswell' I: 146
    'Slieve Donard' I: 22, **146–147**; II: 146
Megascea II: 170
Moorea II: 116
Mucuna sloanei II: 26
***Myrtus apiculata* 'Glanleam Gold'** I: 19, **114–115**
  luma I: 114

Narcissus I: 20, 174, 178; II: 14
  'Arctic Gold' I: 21
  'Beersheba' I: 178
  'Bishop Mann' I: 21
  'Camelot' I: 182
  'Cantatrice' I: 21, **178–179**; II: 190, 206
  'Colleen Bawn' I: 21, 178
  'Crocus' I: 182
  cyclamineus II: 190
  'Foundling' II: **190–191**, 206
  'Kelpie' II: 190
  'Kingscourt' I: 21, **182–183**; II: 190, 206
  'Lavender Lass' I: 182
  'Leda' I: 178
  'Lilac Charm' I: 182
  'Lucifer' II: 134
  'Olympic Gold' I: 21, 182
  'Pink Champagne' I: 182
  'Pink Gin' I: 182
  'Rose of Tralee' I: 182
  'Royalist' I: 182
  'Salmon Trout' I: 182
  'Trinity College Maximus' II: 14
Neomoorea I: 222; II: 116
Nepenthes rajah I: 29, 170
Nerine II: 158, 162
  bowdenii II: 158
  'Cortusa' II: 158
  'Glensavage Gem' II: **158–159**
  'Guy Fawkes' II: 158
  'John Fanning' II: **158–159**
  sarniensis II: 158
  'Silchester Rose' II: 158
  'The Giraffe' II: 158
  'The Spider' II: 158
  'Tweedledee' II: 158
  'Tweedledum' II: 158

Odontoglossum I: 222
Oenothera II: 62
  drummondii I: 25
Olearia I: 22, 27
  chathamica II: 102
  'Henry Travers' II: **102–103**
  'Rossii' I: 19
  semidentata II: 102
  traversii I: 27; II: 104
Orobanche rubra I: 12
Otanthus maritimus I: **78–79**
Ouvirandra fenestralis II: 13
Oxalis acetosella II: **46–47**
  corniculata II: 46
Oxypetalum coeruleum II: **94–95**

Pachystegia insignis II: 15
***Paeonia* 'Anne Rosse'** I: 23, **122–123**
  cambesedesii II: 132
  delavayi I: 122
  lutea I: 122
    var. *ludlowii* I: 122
  suffruticosa I: 122
Pancratium II: 106
***Papaver* 'Fireball'** II: **186–187**
  lateritium II: 186
  orientale II: 186
  'Nanum Flore Pleno' II: 186
  pseudo-orientale II: 186
Pelargonium II: 194
  alchemilloides II: 194
  capitatum II: 194
  'Koko' II: 8, **194–196**
  'Mexicana' II: 194
  'Mexican Beauty' II: 194
  'Mexikanerin' II: 194
  peltatum II: 194
  'Rio Grande' II: 196
  'Rouletta' II: 194
Penstemon fruticosus I: 186
  var. *scouleri* I: 26, 186
    'Alba' I: **186–187**
  scouleri I: 26, 186
Philadelphus coulteri I: 26
Phlox drummondii I: 25
Phragmites II: 22
Phyllostachys stauntonii II: 122
Pieris formosa 'Rowallane' I: 138; II: 178
Pilea wattersii I: 29
Pinguicula grandiflora I: 13, 20, 26, **70–72**; II: 34, 38
  lusitanica I: 70
  × *scullyi* I: 70; II: 38
  vulgaris I: 70, 72; II: 38
Pinus coulteri I: 26, 192
Pittosporum tenuifolium I: 150
  'Lustre' I: 150
  'Silver Queen' I: **150–151**; II: 146
  'Tricolor' I: 150
Polygonum chinense II: 122
Potentilla davurica I: 134
  'Daydawn' I: 134
  'Donard Gold' I: 134
  fruticosa I: 10, **42–43**, 134
  'Longacre' I: 42
  'Manchu' I: 134
  'Sophie's Blush' I: **134–135**
  'Tangerine' I: 22, 42, 134
Primula 'Aileen Aroon' II: 174
  auricula I: 110
  bhutanica II: 82
  'Celtic King' I: 110
  chungensis II: 174
  × *chunglenta* II: 174
  'Duke of Beaufort' I: 110
  'Dutch Triumph' I: 110
  edgeworthii II: 8, **82–83**, 86
  gracilipes II: 82
  hirsuta I: 110
  japonica II: 174
    'Lissadell Pink' II: 174
    'Molly Malone' II: 174
    obconica I: 29
    petiolaris II: 82
    var. *edgeworthii* II: 82
    var. *pulverulenta* II: 82
  × ***pubescens* 'Old Irish Blue'** I: **110–111**
  pulverulenta II: 174
  'Queen Alexandra' I: 110
  'Red Hugh' II: 174
  'Rowallane Rose' I: 20, 138; II: 146, **174–175**, 178
  'Royal Pair' I: 110
  'Royal Widow' I: 110
  'Rufus' I: 110
  sinensis I: 29, 198
  sonchifolia II: 82
  veris I: 11, **82–83**; II: 78
  vulgaris II: **78–79**
    'Elizabeth Dickey' II: **78–79**
  whitei II: 82
Prunus II: 202
  'Kanzan' II: 202
  laurocerasus II: 202
  microlepis var. *smithii* II: 202
  miqueliana II: 202
  padus II: 202
  spinosa II: 202
  ***subhirtella* 'Autumnalis'** II: 8, **202–203**

Ranunculus II: 70, 74
Rhododendron I: 22; II: 154
  aperantum II: 142
  arboreum I: 166
    'Album' I: 166
    'Fernhill' I: 18, 166–167; II: 142
    'Fernhill Silver' I: **166–167**; II: 142
    'Mrs Darley' I: 166
  augustinii I: 30, **214–215**
  auriculatum I: 214
  barbatum I: 18
  'Buccaneer' I: 166
  burmanicum I: 31, **218–219**
  cuffeanum I: 31, 218
  euchaites II: 142

'Evelyn Slinger' II: 142, **146–147**
griersonianum II: 142
hypoglaucum I: 214
'Irish Beauty' II: 142
'Joan Slinger' II: 146
'Kenlis' II: 142
'Lady Dunleath' II: 142
maddenii I: 28
meddianum II: 142
'Mulroy Vanguard' II: **142–143**
'Nigel Marshall' II: 142
orbiculare II: 142
'Redstart' II: 142
'Rosealind Slinger' II: 146
'Sangreal' II: 142
'Scarletta' I: 166
'Thomas Bolas' I: 166; II: 142
thomsonii var. *grandiflorum* II: 142
'Vanguard' II: 142
venator II: 142
yakusimanum II: 146
Ribes I: 158
Romneya coulteri I: 26, **190–192**; II: 116
trichocalyx I: 190
Rosa 'Ards Rover' II: 208
'Arthur Bell' I: 21
bracteata II: **122–123**
canina I: 16; II: 18, 20
ssp. *dumetorum* II: 20
'Crimson Glory' I: 21
'Dame Edith Helen' II: 208
'Dickson's Flame' II: 206
'Earl of Dufferin' II: 206
'Elizabeth of Glamis' I: 21
'Ena Harkness' I: 21
'Gentle Touch' II: 206
'Grandpa Dickson' II: 206
'Handel' II: 206
× ***hibernica*** I: 12, 16; II: 8, **18–20**, 22, 208
'Irish Beauty' II: 208
'Irish Brightness' II: 208
'Irish Elegance' II: **206–208**
'Irish Engineer' II: 208
'Irish Glory' II: 208
'Irish Harmony' II: 208
'Irish Modesty' II: 208
'Irish Pride' II: 208
'Irish Star' II: 208
'Killarney' II: 208
'Lady Helen Stewart' II: 206
macartnea II: 122
'Miss Ethel Brownlow' II: 206
'Mrs Sam McGredy' II: 206
'Peek-a-boo' II: 206
'Picasso' II: 206
'Piccadilly' II: 206
pimpinellifolia I: 16; II: 18, 20
'Red Devil' II: 206
'Rose of Tralee' II: 206
'Silver Lining' II: 208
'Souvenir de La Malmaison' I: 130
'Souvenir de Saint Anne's' I: 17, **130–131**; II: 206
Rubus cockburnianus II: 126
fruticosus II: 126
idaeus II: 126
lasiostylus II: **126–127**
reflexus II: 122
× *vedrariensis* II: 126

Sambucus nigra II: 166
'Albomarginata' II: 166
'Aurea' II: 166
'Aureomarginata' II: 166
'Foliis Purpureis' II: 166
'Guincho Purple' II: **166–167**
f. *laciniata* II: 166
f. *porphyrophylla* II: **166–167**
'Purpurea' II: 166
'Purpureus' II: 166
Sandersonia II: 110
Sarracenia flava I: 25, 74, 76
leucophylla I: 76
× *moorei* I: 76
× *popei* I: 76
purpurea I: **74–76**
rubra I: 76
Saxifraga II: 16, 170
sect. Robertsoniana II: 34
'Ballawley Guardsman' II: 170
hirsuta II: **34–36**
hypnoides II: 34
oppositifolia II: 34
× ***polita*** II: **34–36**
rosacea II: 34
spathularis I: 9; II: **34–36**
umbrosa II: 36
× *urbium* II: 34
Scilla verna I: 8; II: **54–55**
Scottia II: 116
Sida picta II: 13
Simethis planifolia I: 14, **62–63**
Sisyrinchium angustifolium II: **66–67**
bermudiana II: 66
graminoides II: 66
hibernicum II: 66
Solanum crispum I: 162
'Autumnale' I: 162
'Glasnevin' I: 20, **162–163**
dulcamara I: 162
melongena I: 162
tuberosum I: 162
Sorbus aria I: 34
aucuparia I: 34
graeca I: 34
hibernica I: **34–35**
Stauntonia II: 122

Tanacetum parthenium 'Rowallane' I: 138; II: 178
Taxus baccata I: 106–108
'Fastigiata' I: 16, **106–108**
'Lutea' I: **106–108**
Testudinaria elephantipes II: 15
Thalictrum II: 74
Todea barbara II: 15
Traversia II: 104
Trichomanes speciosum I: **50–51**; II: 16
Trifolium dubium II: 46
pratensis II: 46
repens II: 46
Trochetia blackburniana II: 16
boutonii II: 16
Trollius II: 16, 74
asiaticus II: 70
europaeus II: **70–71**, 74
'Orangeman' II: 70
'Prince of Orange' II: 70
Tweedia coerulea II: 94
versicolor II: 94

Ulex downiensis I: 102
europaeus I: 98, **102–104**; II: 58
'Flore Pleno' I: 102
'Strictus' I: **102–104**
gallii I: 102
strictus I: 102

Velleia salmoniana II: 15, 116
Veronica II: 154
headfortii II: 154
Viburnum I: 198
henryi I: 198
opulus I: 198
plicatum f. *tomentosum* I: 198
'Rowallane' I: 198; II: 178
propinquum I: 198
rhytidophyllum I: 198
sargentii I: 198
utile I: 29, **198–199**

Wahlenbergia hederacea II: 42
Weigela I: 194
Wisteria sinensis II: 15

Xanthorrhoea II: 14

Zygopetalum mackayi II: 13

(2) People, places and common names of plants

Abercorn, Duke and Duchess of I: 134
Nursery I: 42, 134
Achill Island II: 28
Adair, Miss Nora I: 22, 142
aiteann gallda – see *Ulex europaeus*
Aiton, William II: 122, 130
Allman, Prof. G.J. I: 78
Prof. William I: 13; II: 116
Amherst, Lady Sarah I: 27, 31
Andes I: 162; II: 34
Andrews, William I: 50, 62
anemone, St Brigid's – see *Anemone coronaria*
wood – see *Anemone nemorosa*
Annaghmakerrig II: 184
Annes Grove I: 19; II: 174
Antrim (county) I: 21, 50, 178; II: 22, 66, 78, 100, 122, 190
Aran Islands I: 46; II: 30, 50, 62
Ardglass II: 54
Ardilaun, Lord I: 17, 130
Lady I: 19, 130
Ardnagashel I: 114
Argentine II: 94
Armagh (county) I: 34; II: 206
Arnold Arboretum I: 198
Ashbourne House, Glounthaune I: 146; II: 138
Athy II: 186
Atlantic Ocean II: 26, 28
auricula – see *Primula* × *pubescens*
Australia I: 26–28; II: 13
Avondale I: 16, 31
Azara, J.N. II: 138
Azores I: 98

Babington, Charles I: 92; II: 50
Baily, Katherine I: 11, 13, 102
Bain, John II: 14
bainne bó bleacht – see *Primula vulgaris*
bainne bó bleachtáin – see *Primula veris*
bainne caoin – see *Euphorbia hyberna*
Balfour, Prof. J.H. I: 94
Ball, Charles Frederick I: 20, 158, 170
Ballard, Mrs Pat I: 126
Ballawley Nursery I: 98; II: 170
Ballinrobe II: 198
Ballsbridge Botanic Garden – see Dublin, Trinity College
Ballyfin II: 186
Ballymoney II: 78
Ballywalter II: 142
Banks, Sir Joseph I: 25; II: 122
Baronscourt I: 134
Barry, T.A. I: 76
Barton, Hugh I: 174
Bartram, John I: 24–25; II: 98, 100
William II: 98
Beamish, Richard I: 146; II: 138
Bean, W.J. I: 20
Bedford, Frederick I: 174
Beijing II: 122
Belfast I: 138; II: 18, 62
Botanic Garden I: 16, 23, 25; II: 114
Belgrove I: 19; II: 138
Ben Bulben I: 10, 38
Benevenagh Mountain I: 38
Bergen, K.A. von II: 170
Bergin, Thomas Fleming I: 94
Bermuda II: 66
bíoma bán – see *Sorbus hibernica*
Birr Castle I: 31, 118, 122
Blakeways-Phillips, Revd R.J. I: 176
Blinkworth, R. I: 194; II: 82
Booth, Evelyn II: 74
Bordeaux II: 11
Borneo I: 20, 23, 28–29, 170
Borrer, William II: 50
Boskoop II: 186
boslelie – see *Crinum moorei*
Botanical Magazine II: 13, 62, 102, 106, 130
Bowles, Edward Augustus II: 74, 90
William I: 98
Brandon Mountain II: 42
Brazil II: 94
broom – see *Cytisus*
Broughshane I: 178
Brown, Robert II: 86, 116
Browne, Dr Patrick I: 11, 12; II: 198
Buddle, Revd Adam II: 86
Bunclody II: 74
Burbidge, Frederick I: 20, 23, 28–29, 170; II: 14–16, 116, 150
Burma I: 134, 166, 178, 218; II: 178
Burren I: 8, 10, 38, 42, 46, 54, 70; II: 30, 34, 46, 74
Butler, Isaac I: 11
butterfly bush – see *Buddleja*
butterwort, greater – see *Pinguicula grandiflora*
Byrne, R. II: 15

cabaiste an mhadra rua – see *Saxifraga spathularis*
cainneann – see *Allium babingtonii*
Calcutta Botanic Garden I: 27; II: 82
California I: 25–26, 190
tree poppy – see *Romneya coulteri*
Cambridge, University of II: 16
Campbell, Andrew I: 17, 130
Canada I: 25, 74
Candolle, Augustin-Pyramus de I: 26, 190
Cape of Good Hope I: 28; II: 106, 110, 194
Carlow (county) I: 50
Carna I: 90
Carncairn Daffodils II: 190
Carnmoney I: 138
Carrickfergus II: 100
Carrigdale Nursery, Newcastle II: 146
Carrowmore, Lough II: 58
Cassells, Prof. Alan II: 194, 196
Judy II: 196
Castlemaine II: 28
Castlewellan I: 17, 19
ceadharlach Bealtaine – see *Gentiana verna*
Celbridge I: 11, 82; II: 46
Chalmers, David II: 78
Chatham Islands I: 27; II: 102
daisy-bush – see *Olearia* 'Henry Travers'
Chelsea Physic Garden II: 9, 130
Chemys, Dr Charles II: 11
cherry, October – see *Prunus subhirtella* 'Autumnalis'
Chile I: 162, 198; II: 62, 118
China I: 42, 122, 166, 202, 206; II: 90, 122, 126, 130, 170, 182
cib ghorm – see *Carex buxbaumii*
cinquefoil, shrubby – see *Potentilla fruticosa*
Clare (county) I: 8, 28, 34, 38, 42, 54, 88; II: 30, 62, 66, 74
Clement, Dr William II: 11
climbing bell – see *Littonia modesta*
Clonee Loughs II: 66
Clonsilla II: 38
Clontarf I: 106, 130
Cloughjordan II: 184
Coey, James I: 22, 150, 178
Coleraine I: 21, 178
Colgan, Nathaniel I: 16
Collinson, Peter I: 24–25, 98; II: 98
Collon I: 16
Comeragh Mountains II: 36
Commerson, Philibert II: 154
Congreve, Ambrose I: 22
Connemara I: 90, 92, 94, 98, 102; II: 58
Cookstown I: 22, 30, 142, 202
Cooper, Roland II: 82
Cork, Botanic Garden I: 13, 16, 23, 26, 70
(county) I: 19, 21, 50, 66, 70, 88, 102, 114, 146; II: 34, 36, 66, 74, 134, 138, 174
University College II: 8, 18, 196, 198
Cornwall I: 78, 94; II: 25, 50, 54
Corrib, Lough I: 42
Corsica II: 132
Cottingham, Capt. Edward II: 118
cottonweed – see *Otanthus maritimus*
Coulter, Dr Thomas I: 23, 190, 192; II: 116
cowslip – see *Primula veris*
Cox, Peter I: 126
cranesbill, bloody – see *Geranium sanguineum*
crann caithne – see *Arbutus unedo*
Crawford, W.H. II: 198
Crimea I: 174
crobh dearg – see *Geranium sanguineum*
Cronk, Dr Quentin II: 16
Cuilcagh Mountain I: 106
cuilean – see *Ilex*
cuinche – see *Arbutus unedo*
Cunningham, George I: 16, 106
Curle, Dr Alexander I: 146
Currey, Miss Fanny II: 74
Curtis, William II: 62

Dabeoc, Saint I: 98
heath – see *Daboecia cantabrica*
daffodil – see *Narcissus*
daisy-bush – see *Olearia*
Daisy Hill Nursery, Newry I: 22, 118, 158; II: 8, 70, 76, 150, 170, 202
Dardanelles I: 20
Dargle Glen I: 22, 31
Darley, Mrs Edmund I: 166
Darwin, Charles I: 20, 72
David, Père Armand I: 23, 29, 210
Delany, Mrs Mary I: 15
Delville I: 15
Dereen I: 19, 114
Derrynane I: 14, 62; II: 26
Devon II: 54
Dickey, Elizabeth II: 78
Dickie, Prof. George I: 14
Mrs Marjorie I: 146
Dickson, Alexander II: 206
George II: 206
Hugh II: 206
Patrick II: 206, 208
Dicksons of Hawlmark I: 21; II: 8, 158, 206, 208
Dingle II: 62
Dixon, Prof. Henry H. II: 15, 34
Samuel I: 110
Dobbs, Arthur I: 24–25; II: 98, 100
Don, David II: 94, 98
Donabate II: 132
Donegal (county) I: 22, 38, 50, 54, 66, 102; II: 30, 36, 66, 70, 142, 174
Doneraile II: 74
Dorrien-Smith, Capt. Arthur II: 102
Dorset I: 94
Douglas, David I: 23, 25–26, 186
dove tree – see *Davidia involucrata*
Dowd, Michael II: 14
Down (county) I: 19, 22; II: 38, 54, 146, 166, 174, 206
Doyle, Dr Gerry II: 58
Drummond, James I: 13, 23, 26–27, 70
James Lawson I: 13
Thomas I: 23, 25, 27, 29
Dublin (county) II: 54, 150
Florists' Club I: 110
National Botanic Gardens, Glasnevin I: 12, 14, 16, 20, 27–28, 31, 50, 72, 74, 76, 94, 102, 106, 114, 118, 122, 130, 158, 166, 170, 190, 194, 210, 218, 222; II: 12, 16, 22, 62, 86, 94, 102, 106, 110, 134, 142, 158, 182, 198
Royal Dublin Society I: 16, 24, 26, 186; II: 100, 110, 118
Trinity College (including College Botanic Garden) I: 13, 16, 20–21, 23, 24, 26, 28, 50, 62, 66, 92, 98, 110, 166, 170, 178, 190; II: 8–16, 22, 34, 58, 110, 114, 116, 118, 130, 182, 194
University College I: 202
duchosach – see *Adiantum capillus-veneris*
Duncan, Brian II: 190
Dundalk I: 26, 190
Dufferin, Lady I: 106
Dunganstown II: 182

Edgeworth, Maria II: 84, 86
Michael Pakenham II: 8, 82, 84, 86
Richard Lovell II: 86
Edgeworthstown II: 82, 86
Edinburgh, Royal Botanic Garden II: 9–10, 182
Royal Scottish Museum I: 146
Edrom Nursery I: 146
elder – see *Sambucus nigra*
Ellis, John II: 98, 100
Elwes, Henry J. I: 31, 106
English Channel II: 76
Enniskerry I: 22
Enniskillen, Earl of I: 16, 106
Eriugena, Johannes Scotus II: 60
Errisbeg Mountain I: 13, 90; II: 58

Fanning, John II: 158
Fanore II: 26
Farges, Père Paul I: 23, 30, 212
Farrer, Reginald I: 31, 134
féasóg na lao – see *Dryas octopetala*
feileastrom – see *Iris pseudoacorus*
feilistrín gorm – see *Sisyrinchium angustifolium*
Ferguson, Dr I.K. II: 130
Mrs L.F. II: 130
Fermanagh (county) I: 38, 50, 90, 106; II: 30, 66, 70
Fernhill I: 18, 166; II: 142
fern, Killarney – see *Trichomanes speciosum*
maidenhair – see *Adiantum capillus-veneris*
Findlater, Miss Doris II: 158, 160
Finn, River II: 70
fiuise – see *Fuchsia magellanica*
Florence I: 76
Florencecourt I: 16, 106, 108
yew – see *Taxus baccata* 'Fastigiata'
flytrap, Venus – see *Dionaea muscipula*
Foley, Cormac II: 184
Ford, Charles I: 202
Forrest, George I: 20, 31
Mary II: 142
Fortune, Robert I: 29
Foss, Dr Peter II: 58
Foster, John I: 16, 102
Fota I: 17
France II: 58
fraoch camogach – see *Erica erigena*
Mhic Aoidh – see *Erica mackaiana*
na h-aon choise – see *Daboecia cantabrica*
Fraser, James I: 16–17
Fuchs, Leonhard I: 7; II: 46, 64
furze – see *Ulex europaeus*

Galtee Mountains II: 36
Galway (county) I: 38, 42, 46, 66, 90, 98; II: 30, 36, 42, 50, 66, 122
Garinish Island – see Ilnacullin
Gartan, Lough II: 70
Geashill II: 136
geelklokkie – see *Littonia modesta*
gentian – see *Gentiana verna*
Geoghegan, Miss Fanny II: 130, 132
Gerard, John I: 8; II: 30, 46, 70
Gill, Lough I: 88
Glanleam I: 18–19, 114; II: 62, 64
Glasgow, University of I: 25, 186
Glasnevin – see Dublin, National Botanic Gardens
Glengarriff I: 88, 114
Glen of the Downs Nursery I: 19, 114
Glenveagh I: 22; II: 142
globe-flower – see *Trollius europaeus*
Gore-Booth, Sir Josslyn II: 174
gorse – see *Ulex europaeus*
Göttingen I: 142
Goulding, Sir Basil I: 22
grass, blue-eyed – see *Sisyrinchium angustifolium*
Guernsey II: 158
lily – see *Nerine*

Guincho II: 166
Gumbleton, William Edward I: 19, 20, 170; II: 138, 158, 162, 184, 198

Hamilton, C.R. I: 138
Lady Sophie I: 134
Hamwood I: 138, 206
Hance, Henry I: 30
handkerchief tree – see *Davidia involucrata*
harebell – see *Campanula rotundifolia*
Harkness, Jack II: 208
Harlow, James I: 15
Hartland, William Baylor I: 21, 178; II: 134, 136, 138, 190
Harvey, Prof. William H. I: 13, 14, 23, 26–29, 62, 190; II: 14, 15, 110, 114, 116
hawkweed – see *Hieracium scullyi*
Haxton, John II: 122
hazel, Chinese witch – see *Hamamelis mollis*
Hayes, Revd F.C. II: 158
Samuel I: 16
Headfort I: 20; II: 142, 154
Marquis of I: 20; II: 142, 154
heath, Dorset – see *Erica ciliaris*
Irish – see *Erica erigena*
Mackay's – see *Erica mackaiana*
St Dabeoc's – see *Daboecia cantabrica*
Heaton, Revd Richard I: 8, 10, 38, 46; II: 54
Helen's Bay II: 166
Henry, Dr Augustine I: 23, 30–31, 106, 198, 202, 206, 210, 212, 214; II: 90, 126, 182
Hermann, P. II: 10
Heslop-Harrison, Prof. J. II: 18
Hill, Prof. Edward II: 12, 13
Hillier, Sir Harold II: 166
Himalaya I: 27–28, 31, 42, 166, 194; II: 82, 86, 170
Himalayan poppy – see *Meconopsis × sheldonii*
Hind, Revd W.H. II: 64
Hodgins, Edward II: 8, 182, 184
John II: 184
Robert II: 182, 184
William II: 184
Holland II: 186
holly – see *Ilex × altaclerensis*
Holywood II: 18
Hong Kong I: 202
Hooker, Sir Joseph I: 19, 30, 166; II: 82, 104, 106
Sir William Jackson I: 25, 28, 50, 62, 92, 190; II: 22, 94, 110
honeysuckle, golden – see *Lonicera tragophylla*
Hornibrook, Murray II: 186
How, William I: 8, 46, 66, 86; II: 54
Howat, Robert II: 166
Howth II: 134
Hubei I: 198, 214; II: 90, 126
Hutchins, Miss Ellen I: 13

Iberian Peninsula II: 34, 50, 54, 58
Ilnacullin I: 19
Inishboffin II: 42
Inishmaan II: 30
Innes, Robert I: 38
Issaquah I: 126
iúr – see *Taxus baccata*

Jackson, Dr Peter Wyse II: 16
Jacquemont, Victor I: 27
Jamaica I: 23–24; II: 198
Japan I: 122, 138, 206; II: 202
Jekyll, Miss Gertrude I: 19
Johnston, Robert II: 18

Keit, Wilhelm I: 76; II: 110
Keogh, Revd John I: 11; II: 30
Kerry (county) I: 19, 50, 62, 66, 70, 78, 114; II: 28, 34, 38, 42, 64, 66, 114
Knight of I: 18; II: 64
lily– see *Simethis planifolia*
Kesteven, Lord I: 202
Kew, Royal Botanic Gardens I: 19, 27, 31, 162, 198, 202, 206, 210, 214, 218, 222; II: 62, 102, 106, 114, 122, 126, 130, 166, 186, 198, 202
Kildare (county) I: 82; II: 134, 186
Kilkenny (county) I: 31; II: 42
Killarney I: 50, 86; II: 34, 184
fern – see *trichomanes speciosum*
Killyleagh I: 23
Kilmacurragh I: 18, 20
Kilruddery I: 15, 110
Kirstenbosch Botanic Gardens II: 110
Knap Hill Nursery I: 138
Knocktopher I: 31

Lady Island Lake I: 78
Lakelands (Cork) II: 198
Lamb, Dr J.G.D. I: 74
Lambay Island II: 42
Lambert, Aylmer Bourke II: 122
Michael I: 94
Langrishe, Revd Sir Hercules I: 31
Laois (county) II: 42, 186
Lawrenson, Mrs Alice Louisa II: 14, 134, 136
Lawson, Messrs II: 184
L'Ecluse, Charles de I: 74; II: 9, 70
leek, Babington's – see *Allium babingtonii*
Leichtlin, Max II: 110
Leiden, University of I: 7, 12; II: 9–11, 14, 86
Leitrim (county) II: 30, 66
Earl of II: 142
leolach – see *Trollius europaeus*
Levinge, Godfrey I: 74
Leyrath I: 31
Lhuyd, Edward I: 9–11, 13, 38, 42, 98; II: 30, 34, 58
Lidstone, Desmond II: 26
Roger II: 26
lily, climbing – see *Littonia modesta*
Guernsey – see *Nerine*
Kerry – see *Simethis planifolia*
Moore's – see *Crinum moorei*
Limerick (county) I: 27–28, 50, 66; II: 102
Lindley, Dr John I: 186
Linnaeus, Carl II: 50, 86, 98
Linton, Revd W.R. II: 38
Lismore II: 74
Lissadell I: 21; II: 174
Litton, Prof. Samuel II: 8, 110
Liverpool I: 16, 106; II: 182, 184
Lobb, William II: 118
Logan, James II: 86
London I: 17; II: 182
Londonderry (county) I: 38; II: 22
Lady I: 19; II: 208
Longford (county) II: 82, 86
Louth (county) I: 190
Lurgan II: 86
Lusitanian plants I: 8–9, 13, 62, 70; II: 34
lus na gaoithe – see *Anemone nemorosa*
na seabhac – see *Hieracium scullyi*
Lynan, James II: 66

McCalla, William I: 90, 92, 94, 186
McCann, Sean II: 206
Macartney, Lord II: 122
McClintock, David II: 58
McGredy, Samuel I: 21; II: 206
McHugh, George II: 136
McIlhenny, Henry P. I: 22; II: 142
McIlwaine, E. I: 138
Mackay, James Townsend I: 13–14, 26, 50, 62, 88, 90, 92, 94, 102; II: 8, 13, 16, 28, 58, 114, 118, 184
heath – see *Erica mackaiana*
McKennedy, D. II: 15
Mackie, Mrs Vera II: 166
McMahon, Bernard I: 154
MacNabb, Mrs Winifred I: 31, 218
Macnean, Lough II: 70
Madden, Major Edward I: 23, 27–28, 194; II: 82, 86
Madeira I: 150; II: 182
maidenhair fern – see *Adiantum capillus-veneris*
Majorca II: 13, 130
Malahide Castle I: 22, 126; II: 130
Malinbeg II: 26
Mangerton Mountain II: 34
Maple, William II: 11
Maries, Charles I: 29, 206
Massey, Major Eyre I: 174
Masters, Dr M.T. II: 198
Mathew, Brian II: 186
Mathias, Brigadier & Mrs I: 176
matilija – see *Romneya coulteri*
Mauritius II: 16
Maymyo Botanic Garden I: 31, 218
Mayo (county) I: 42, 66, 74, 90, 98; II: 30, 36, 58, 198
mearacan gorm – see *Campanula rotundifolia*
Meath (county) I: 20, 34, 206; II: 142, 154
Earl of I: 110
Meikle, R. Desmond II: 166
Melvin, Lough II: 70
Menzies, Archibald I: 25, 28
Mexico I: 25; II: 46
Micholitz, Wilhelm I: 222
Mitchelstown I: 11
Moira I: 15, 16; II: 166
Molyneux, Sir Thomas I: 9–12, 24; II: 10, 34
William I: 9, 24
Monaghan (county) II: 184
Moore, Charles I: 118; II: 13
Dr David I: 14, 17, 20, 27, 72, 76, 118, 166, 194, 222; II: 8, 13–14, 22, 86, 106, 116
Sir Frederick I: 17, 19–22, 31, 130, 158, 218, 222; II: 14, 102, 116, 150, 154
Hugh Armytage I: 20, 138; II: 154, 178
Revd John I: 138
Lady Phylis I: 130, 138; II: 138, 150, 202
moran giobach – see *Saxifraga hirsuta*
More, Alexander Goodman I: 14; II: 42
Morris, Megan II: 74
mountain avens – see *Dryas octopetala*
Mount Congreve I: 22, 31
Mount Stewart I: 19, 102, 166; II: 142, 174, 178, 208
Mount Usher I: 17, 20, 26, 31, 118, 166, 194; II: 138, 154
Mourne Mountains I: 102
Mueller, Ferdinand von II: 15
Mullet Peninsula II: 58
Mulligan, Brian II: 174
Mulroy II: 142, 174
Mweelrea Mountain II: 58

Nacung, Lough I: 90
Natal II: 110, 114
Neagh, Lough II: 22
Nelson, Dr E. Charles II: 58, 146
Nenagh I: 176; II: 162
Newcastle (County Down) I: 22, 134; II: 146
Newtownards I: 19, 102; II: 206, 208
New Zealand I: 27–28, 150, 186; II: 13, 62, 102, 104, 154, 206
Nicholson, Prof. Henry II: 10–11
Niven, Ninian I: 16–17; II: 13, 94
Norris, Tony II: 158
North Carolina I: 24–25; II: 98, 100
North Sea II: 26
Noyer, George du II: 22
Nutt, Richard I: 174, 176
Nuttall, Thomas I: 154
Nymans I: 118, 122

O'Connell, Daniel I: 62
O'Donoghue, Rory I: 86
Offaly (county) I: 74, 118, 122; II: 42, 136
Oliver, Daniel I: 206
Omagh I: 146; II: 190
O'Mahony, Revd Thaddeus I: 14, 62
Ordnance Survey II: 22
Orkney Islands I: 38; II: 54
Ouden, H. den II: 186
Outer Hebrides II: 26, 54
Oxford, University of II: 9, 11

Parkinson, John I: 8
Parnell, William II: 16
Patrick, Saint II: 46
Patten, Hugo I: 146
peasairim thra – see *Lathyrus japonicus*
pea, sea – see *Lathyrus japonicus* ssp. *maritimus*
Pelargonium Petal Streak Agent II: 194, 196
Penn, William II: 86
Pennell, F.W. II: 154
Petiver, John II: 11
Philadelphia I: 24, 154; II: 86, 98
Pisa I: 7
pitcher-plant – see *Sarracenia purpurea*
Plumier, Charles I: 24
Poë, Miss Blanche II: 162
James Hill I: 18, 176; II: 162
John Thomas Bennett I: 176; II: 162
Pope, William I: 76
poppy – see *Papaver*
blue – see *Meconopsis × sheldonii*
California tree – see *Romneya coulteri*
Himalayan – see *Meconopsis × sheldonii*
Portadown II: 206
potatoes I: 11
Powerscourt I: 17, 106
Praeger, Mrs Hedi I: 98
Robert Lloyd I: 14, 98
primrose – see *Primula vulgaris*
candelabra – see *Primula* 'Rowallane Rose'
Edgeworth's – see *Primula edgeworthii*

Qianlong, Emperor II: 122
Queen's University, Belfast I: 29–30, 198; II: 18
Quin I: 88
quince – see *Chaenomeles × superba*

Rawdon, Sir Arthur I: 15; II: 166
Sir John I: 15
Ray, John I: 66, 98
Reade, Mrs Kate II: 190
Reamsbottom, W. II: 136
Richardson, Lionel I: 21, 182; II: 190
Richmond Nursery I: 154
Ringsend I: 54
Riverston House I: 176
Robinson, Dr David II: 102
Dr Tancred I: 98
Revd Thomas Romney I: 26, 190; II: 116
William I: 17–18, 21; II: 14, 74, 134
Rocky Mountains I: 25, 38, 42
Rodger, McClelland & Co., Newry II: 170
Rogers, Charles II: 178
Roscommon (county) I: 74; II: 11
rose, Irish – see *Rosa × hibernica*
Macartney's – see *Rosa bracteata*
ros gaelach – see *Rosa × hibernica*
Ross of Bladensburg, Sir John I: 19, 188, 198
Ross, Robert II: 60
Rossbeigh II: 28
Rossdohan I: 19; II: 114
Rosse, Earl of I: 22–23, 122
Anne, Countess of I: 122
Rostrevor I: 19, 118, 198
Roundstone I: 90, 92, 94, 98; II: 50
Roughty River II: 38
Rowallane I: 19–20, 22, 138, 198; II: 154, 174, 178, 180
Rowley, G. II: 20
Royal Horticultural Society of Ireland I: 22, 110; II: 118, 158, 162, 170
Royal Horticultural Society [of London] I: 15, 18, 21, 22, 118, 122, 126, 138, 142, 150, 154, 162, 174, 176, 178, 182; II: 118, 134, 136, 150, 158, 166, 170, 178, 184, 190, 208
Royle, John I: 27
Russell, John I: 154
Rutherfoord, Miss Rita II: 158
Rutty, Dr John I: 11–12

sadhbhóg sḣléibhe – see *Pinguicula grandiflora*
St Anne's, Clontarf I: 17, 130
St Albans I: 222
St Brigid – see Mrs A.L. Lawrenson
St Brigid's anemone – see *Anemone coronaria*
St Helena II: 16
St John's wort – see *Hypericum*
Salmon, Dr George II: 15, 116
Sanders, Messrs I: 222
Sanderson, John II: 110, 114
Dr Molly II: 74, 78
Sardinia II: 132
Sargent, Dr Charles I: 198
Savill, Sir Eric I: 154
Scannell, Miss M.J.P. I: 90
Scilly, Isles of I: 78; II: 102
sciolla earraigh – see *Scilla verna*
Scotland I: 50, 74, 146, 202; II: 22, 94, 150, 166
Scott, Prof. Robert II: 12–13, 114
Scouler, Dr John I: 25–26, 186
Scully, Dr Reginald I: 70; II: 34, 38
seamrog – see shamrock
seamsog – see *Oxalis acetosella*
sedge, club – see *Carex buxbaumii*
seilistrom – see *Iris pseudoacorus*
Shackleton, David I: 176
Lydia I: 222
shamrock I: 8, 11; II: 46
Shaw-Smith, Desmond II: 170
Shepherd, John II: 182, 184
Sherard, James I: 66
Shetland II: 34
singirlini – see *Fuchsia magellanica*
Slattery, Patrick II: 206
Slieve Donard Nursery I: 20, 22, 42, 134, 138, 142, 146, 150, 154, 158, 166, 178; II: 142, 146, 150, 174, 178
Slieve League I: 38
Sligo (county) I: 34, 38, 50, 88; II: 30, 66, 174
Slinger, Leslie I: 22; II: 146, 178
William I: 22
slipperwort – see *Calceolaria × burbidgei*
Sloane, Sir Hans I: 15, 22–23; II: 86
Smith, Dr Charles I: 70; II: 28
Thomas I: 22; II: 8, 170, 202
snowdrops – see *Galanthus*
Solander, Dr Daniel II: 100
sorrel, wood – see *Oxalis acetosella*
South America I: 50; II: 62, 154, 198
Span, Prof. James II: 11
spurge, Irish – see *Euphorbia hyberna*
squill, spring – see *Scilla verna*
Staunton, Sir George II: 122
Stearn, Dr William T. II: 50
Steep Holme II: 50
Stelfox, Arthur II: 22
Stephens, Prof. William I: 66; II: 11, 16, 194
Stern, F.C. I: 174
Stewart, S.A. II: 22
Straffan I: 18, 174
strawberry tree – see *Arbutus unedo*
Stronach, D. II: 122
sugarlini – see *Fuchsia magellanica*
Sydney, Royal Botanic Garden I: 118; II: 13
Sylliard, Zanchie I: 8
Synge, J.M. II: 30
Synnott, Donal M. II: 22

Talbot de Malahide, Viscount I: 22–23, 126; II: 130
Taylor, Dr Thomas I: 13
Templeton, John I: 12–13, 16; II: 18, 54, 62
Thailand II: 13
Thistleton-Dyer, Sir William I: 30
Thomas, Graham Stuart II: 174
Threlkeld, Dr Caleb I: 10–11, 54, 58, 66, 82; II: 42, 46
Tierra del Fuego II: 62
tipitiwitchet – see *Dionaea muscipula*
Tipperary (county) I: 176; II: 36, 66, 162, 184
Tolka, River I: 106
Toomebridge II: 22
Toubol, Very Revd U. II: 74, 76
Tournefort, Joseph de I: 23–24
Tradescant, John I: 74
Travers, Henry Hammersley I: 27; II: 102, 104
William T.L. I: 27; II: 102, 104
Tresco II: 102
Treseder's Nursery I: 114
Trinity College Botanic Garden – see Dublin, University of
Turner, William I: 8
Tweedia – see *Oxypetalum coeruleum*
Tweedie, John II: 94
Tyrone (county) I: 22, 50, 146, 202; II: 190

ubhla caithne – see *Arbutus unedo*
Uniacke, Col. R.L. I: 19, 114
Uruguay II: 94

Valentia Island I: 18, 114; II: 62, 64
Vancouver, Capt. I: 25
Veitch, Messrs I: 28–29, 198, 206, 210; II: 14, 90, 118
Venus fly-trap – see *Dionaea muscipula*
Vesci, Viscountess de I: 76
Victoria, Mount I: 31, 218
Vietnam I: 222
Vilmorin, Maurice de I: 31, 212

Wade, Prof. Walter I: 12, 16, 42, 102; II: 13, 110
Waddy, John I: 78
Wakefield, Edward I: 88
Wales I: 50; II: 54
Walker, Robert II: 142
Mrs Sally II: 142
Wallich, Nathaniel I: 27; II: 82
Walpole, Edward I: 17, 20; II: 154
Ward, Frank Kingdon I: 31, 218
Waterford (county) I: 21, 22, 66, 78, 102, 182; II: 36, 74
Watson, William II: 146
Watson's Nursery, Killiney I: 21, 118; II: 150
Watters, Thomas I: 29–30, 198
Webb, Prof. David I: 14, 88; II: 15, 34, 58, 62
Mr II: 106
West Indies II: 198
Wexford (county) I: 78, 102; II: 54
Wheeler-Cuffe, Lady Charlotte I: 23, 31, 166, 218; II: 178
Sir Otway I: 31
whin – see *Ulex europaeus*
White, John I: 14, 102
whitebeam, Irish – see *Sorbus hibernica*
Wicklow (county) I: 34, 102, 106; II: 36, 182, 184
Wild, S.G. II: 15
Willbrook I: 130
Williams, Laurie II: 26
Willis, Dr David I: 178
George I: 16, 106
Wilson, Ernest I: 30, 198, 202, 210, 212, 214; II: 90
Guy I: 21, 178, 182; II: 190
Windsor I: 154
Wood, Philip I: 42, 134
wood anemone – see *Anemone nemorosa*
sorrel – see *Oxalis acetosella*
Wisley Gardens II: 166
Woodford II: 66
Woods, Joseph II: 22
Wright, Prof. E.P. II: 15

yellow flag – see *Iris pseudoacorus*
yew – see *Taxus baccata*
Yichang I: 29–30, 198, 202, 206, 210, 214
Yorkshire I: 42, 46, 50; II: 166
Young, William II: 98